Would Jesus Christ Do That?

is the first question!

What Would Jesus Do?

is the second question!

Richard W. Linford

A Sweetwater Book Company publication.
Fourth edition

ISBN 1-57574-016-8

Imprint Linford Corporation

Contents

A Sweetwater Book Company publication

Would Jesus Christ Do That?

1 **What will happen to you and to me when Jesus Christ comes in His glory?**

Bishop Bruce James was still in his pajamas at 10 am on Saturday morning, working at his oversized, faux mahogany desk in his study at home.

He was typing on his state of the art computer which was capable of much more than word processing. His children had given it to him including a brand new twenty four inch flat screen monitor. Bishop James didn't use his computer for business applications now that he was retired, although he did use spreadsheets to keep track of his performance in meeting his goals.

He was working on a talk for Sunday and he had been thinking and writing for several days, draft after draft, until finally he was nearly satisfied. His subject was caring for the poor and the needy and his text was taken from Matthew chapter 25:

31 When the Son of man [Jesus Christ] shall come in his glory, and all the holy angels with him, then shall he sit upon the throne of his glory:

32 And before him shall be gathered all nations: and he shall separate them one from another, as a shepherd divideth his sheep from the goats:

33 And he shall set the sheep on his right hand, but the goats on the left.

34 Then shall the King say unto them on his right hand, **Come, ye blessed of my Father, inherit the kingdom prepared for you from the foundation of the world:**

35 **For I was an hungered, and ye gave me meat: I was thirsty, and ye gave me drink: I was a stranger, and ye took me in:**

36 **Naked, and ye clothed me: I was sick, and ye visited me: I was in prison, and ye came unto me.**

37 Then shall the righteous answer him, saying, Lord, when saw we thee an hungred, and fed thee? or thirsty, and gave thee drink?

38. When saw we thee a stranger, and took thee in? or naked, and clothed thee?

39 Or when saw we thee sick, or in prison, and came unto thee?

40 And the King shall answer and say unto them, **Verily I say unto you, Inasmuch as ye have done it unto one of the least of these my brethren, ye have done it unto me.**

41 Then shall he say also unto them on the left hand, **Depart from me, ye cursed, into everlasting fire, prepared for the devil and his angels:**

42 **For I was an hungred, and ye gave me no meat: I was thirsty, and ye gave me no drink:**

43 **I was a stranger, and ye took me not in: naked, and ye clothed me not: sick, and in prison, and ye visited me not.**

44 Then shall they also answer him, saying, Lord, when saw we thee an hungred, or athirst, or a stranger, or naked, or sick, or in prison, and did not minister unto thee?

45 Then shall he answer them, saying, **Verily I say unto you, Inasmuch as ye did it not to one of the least of these, ye did it not to me.**

46 And these shall go away into everlasting punishment: but the righteous into life eternal.

Bishop James felt that this text fit very well with the title he had chosen.

2 What does "In His Steps" mean?

The bishop had taken the title of his talk from a book by Charles Monroe Sheldon who was born in 1857 and died in 1946. This book, now world famous, carried the short title "In His Steps" and was first published in 1896. The little book became one of the best sellers of all time, selling to-date more than 30 million copies.

Though "In His Steps" was a work of fiction, the bishop thought Sheldon's "In His Steps" carried a clear ring of truth. It told the story of the happenstance visit of a thirty-three-year-old, sick and out of work young man to a Reverend Maxwell, first at his home, and then later at his parish during a Sunday service.

After Reverend Maxwell's sermon, the young man caused quite a commotion when he walked from the back to the front of the chapel. There, to the dismay and consternation of the Reverend and his parishioners, the young man took serious time berating the good Reverend and his congregation for not reaching out to help those who are poor and needy.

Within a few days of delivering his scolding lecture, this young and vocal critic died; whereupon, Reverend Maxwell wrote and preached a sermon titled "In His Steps: What Would Jesus Do?"

3 What Would Jesus Do?

Reverend Maxwell's congregation, in response to the Reverend's fine sermon, and in memory of this poor and earnest young man, and also no doubt because a few consciences were stung by the young man's diatribe, promised to ask regularly "What would Jesus do?"

Each member of the congregation including the Reverend and his wife Constance made solemn promises to mend their ways. As an aside, Constance is a great name for Reverend Maxwell's wife because Constance was a model of constant Christian living and service.

As a result of these promises and the intensified efforts on the part of the parish members and a great deal of work on the part of Reverend Maxwell and Constance, the result was much more service to others. From this increased service, over a short period of time, the congregation and the Reverend's family became noticeably more Christ-like.

"In His Steps" rang true to most who read it. And from those 30 million books sold or given away, Mr. Sheldon became a powerful influence for good, an influence far beyond his humble imagination. Throughout the world, millions no doubt still ask that seminal question "What would Jesus do?" And the answer has resulted in and still does result in millions of kindly deeds.

And all of this simply because of Charles Sheldon's articulate and simple plea that men, women, teens and children, ask the question, "What would Jesus do?" and then conduct their lives accordingly. The title Bishop James' gave to his next Sunday sermon was basic enough and not the least bit original. He simply titled his sermon "What would Jesus do?"

4 Are you odd or are you even?

While Bishop James was working on his talk, his wife, who by some interesting coincidence was also named Constance, stopped by his study.

"Bruce," she said, "I have some errands to run." She never called him Bishop. He was simply Bruce and she did that not out of disrespect but out of some notion that it kept him humble if she called him Bruce. "I'm going to the post office, to the chapel to pick up some trays and dishes, to the store for milk and other groceries, to get gas for the car, and then home. I love you. Do you want to pray before I leave?

"Prayer is good," said Bishop Bruce. "It's your day, so you pray," he said.

Since he was odd and she was even tempered, several years back the two of them had reconciled most all of their marital differences in a remarkably effective way simply by assigning even days to her and odd days to him.

On even days she got to decide everything ranging from where they might eat out to what they would do or where they would go for an activity, to what project in the yard or house they worked on together. On the odd days he got to choose everything. On her even days she even got to run the TV remote.

Bruce was not oblivious to the fact that he picked up a couple of extra odd days throughout the year whenever a month had thirty-one days. She noticed as well and called them "his bonus days." Since it was an even day, she prayed:

"Heavenly Father," "We thank thee for our health, for our children and grandchildren, for money to buy what we need, for good Christian work. Please bless us with thy Holy Spirit, with safety, with more holiness, and with greater kindness and ability to serve others. Please bless Bruce as he prepares his talk so his words and actions will encourage and move the members of the ward to a greater state of goodness and service. In the name of Jesus Christ, Amen.

She blew him a kiss, picked up her packages and mail and left. No question she was a great and beautiful lady. Bruce knew this and deeply appreciated her beauty and wisdom, her kindness and spirituality, and her special penchant for service. Her smile was joyful and infectious and members of the congregation gravitated to her, confided in her, and looked up to her.

5 What is it like to have the Holy Spirit speak through you to the benefit of others?

After Constance left, Bruce continued working on his talk.

He practiced reading it out loud.

He had learned long ago that few talks for him were worth any salt unless he practiced.

Notwithstanding, he knew there were times when the Holy Spirit spoke through him, when no amount of thinking or writing or preparation made any difference, when words from his mouth were not his own. At such times he felt that those special words came directly from God with admonition and love for the benefit of God's congregation.

More often than not those in the congregation knew as well when God's spiritual power was manifest to them through Bishop James.

6 Do you think directing someone to your welfare shelter is enough?

More than an hour passed by quickly since Constance left when the doorbell rang.

With absent mindedness of which he knew he was more often than not guilty, and still dressed in his pajamas, reading and verbalizing his talk half under his breath, and thinking it might be one of his children, Bishop James went to the front door only to find on his door step perhaps the most disheveled once good looking young woman he had ever seen in his life.

She looked to be in her early thirties. Her blond hair, though not dirty, was uncut and stringy. She was wearing very old loose fitting faded blue jeans, a thread-bare blue shirt, and an even older somewhat stained red pullover sweater. Her blue eyes were glazed with a distant glassy stare Bruce thought was singular to drug addicts and alcoholics. He had seen that look before; those spaced out flat eyes. He had seen it on any number of young and old people who had come to his door looking for help and a handout.

"My name is Mary," she said.

"Yes, Mary?" he said.

"Mary Thomas," she mumbled. "I heard you are the bishop. I need some food and I need some money." Mary was direct and to the point.

Observing that Mary was standing, mobile, and able to speak, Bishop James countered.

"Mary, our welfare square facility is open over on 780 West 800 South, just one block from here. There is a bishop who provides help to persons in your circumstance. He has access to food through a bishop's storehouse, and clothing through a Deseret Industries thrift store, and employment counseling, and even what we call fast offering funds. He can refer you to a shelter where you can get breakfast, midday, and evening meals. He can refer you to a nurse and doctor for medicine. He can help you with almost any problem including treatment for drug or alcohol abuse or virtually any other need, including as I mentioned perhaps even a small amount of cash.

With an unmistakable note of pride, he continued: "We take turns providing some of the man power to support Welfare Square. Mary, Welfare Square is only a few blocks away. When you get there, ask for Bishop John Major and tell him I sent you."

Bishop James started to close the door.

7 What more could possibly be needed?

Mary looked at him through her half empty eyes. She appeared to grasp what he had said.

Without reply Mary shuffled backwards, turned, and with head down walked with abnormal gait toward 780 West.

Bishop James had done his Christian duty. He had directed this poor and needy and apparently drug-wasted young woman to the welfare center.

Bishop James went back to his study and took up where he left off in the middle of his rehearsal. He was reciting the Savior's words in Matthew 25, when Constance drove in the drive way. She opened the garage and yelled to him. "Bruce, can you help me with the groceries?" Bruce dutifully put away his sermon and walked outside to the car to help carry in the groceries.

"Who was that young woman leaving our house, Bruce?" Constance said with muffled words through the armload of grocery bags she was carrying.

"She said her name is Mary," said Bruce. "She needed help and I directed her to Welfare Square."

In retrospect, and for years after, it would be disconcerting to the good Bishop Bruce James that he had felt no feelings of conscience while talking to Mary. No discomfort. No dissonance, as one might anticipate or expect. No quiet whisperings of the Holy Spirit. No promptings that so often came to him when he did something wrong or failed to do something right. There were simply no feelings one way or another over this brief encounter with Mary. She had asked for his help and he had directed Mary to Welfare Square. He had quietly closed the door and gone back to practicing his talk. What more could possibly be needed?

8 "What Would Jesus Do?"

Sunday came, and it was a mighty hot Sabbath morning in the chapel and getting hotter by the minute. The air conditioner had stopped working that morning.

"After the sacrament was passed, Bishop James stepped to the podium. "I tried to reach a service technician," he explained. "None are available until tomorrow. One yellow page ad promised 24-hour service, but I could not reach the technicians as their answering machine was full. I suppose it makes sense given the fact today is the Sabbath. I apologize for not providing you with air conditioning. My talk is not overly long. Notwithstanding, I invite you men to take off your jackets and you ladies to use the program as a fan. I want you to be as comfortable as possible.

"I have titled my remarks, "What would Jesus do?" is a simple question. It is a profound question of consequence. A question perhaps first minted by Charles Monroe Sheldon who was born in 1857 and died in 1946. A phrase first coined by Charles Sheldon in his now world famous writing titled *"In His Steps."* His little book was first published in 1896 and through the years became one of the best sellers of all time. To date, it has sold more than 30 million copies. *"In His Steps"* is fiction, although I have always thought it was based on a true event. It has a clear and distinct ring of truth. It tells the story of the happenstance visit of a thirty-three-year-old sick, out of work, needy and seedy young man -- first at Reverend Maxwell's home, and then to his parish during a Sunday service.

"After Reverend Maxwell's sermon, the young man caused quite a commotion by walking from the back to the front of the chapel where much to the dismay and consternation of the congregation he took more than thirty minutes berating the good Reverend and his congregation for not reaching out to help those in need. Then, a few short days after delivering his harangue and scolding, the poor young man and critic died.

"Whereupon, the Reverend conducted the funeral and thereafter wrote and preached his masterful sermon, *"In His Steps: What Would Jesus Do?"*

"And Reverend Maxwell's congregation, in memory of this poor, earnest young man, and in response no doubt to many a sharply stung conscience, promised each other that each day, as they faced decisions and choices, they would ask "What would Jesus do?" Each member of the congregation including Reverend Maxwell promised to modify their ways accordingly and the primary result on the part of the members of the congregation and Reverend Maxwell and his wife Constance was in fact much more Christ-like service to others.

"Because of the simple message found in those 30 million books, Charles Sheldon became a powerful influence for good with millions of adults and millions of teens and children. His influence came in a four-word question "What would Jesus do?"

"These millions of acts of service occurred in some significant measure because of Charles Sheldon's heartfelt plea that men, women, and children everywhere ask the question, "What would Jesus do?" and then most importantly do accordingly.

"Today, I commend this same exercise to each of you. When individuals or groups need help, ask the question, "What would Jesus do? And when answering this question, "What would Jesus do?" keep in mind these sobering words from Matthew 25 which outline clearly what his sheep would do; and brothers and sisters, we clearly want to be a congregation of his sheep found on his right hand.

31 When the Son of man shall come in his glory, and all the holy angels with him, then shall he sit upon the throne of his glory:

32 And before him shall be gathered all nations: and he shall separate them one from another, as a shepherd divideth his sheep from the goats:

33 And he shall set the sheep on his right hand, but the goats on the left.

34 Then shall the King say unto them on his right hand, **Come, ye blessed of my Father, inherit the kingdom prepared for you from the foundation of the world:**

35 **For I was an hungered, and ye gave me meat: I was thirsty, and ye gave me drink: I was a stranger, and ye took me in:**

36 **Naked, and ye clothed me: I was sick, and ye visited me: I was in prison, and ye came unto me.**

37 Then shall the righteous answer him, saying, Lord, when saw we thee an hungred, and fed thee? or thirsty, and gave thee drink?

38 When saw we thee a stranger, and took thee in? or naked, and clothed thee?

39 Or when saw we thee sick, or in prison, and came unto thee?

40 And the King shall answer and say unto them, **Verily I say unto you, Inasmuch as ye have done it unto one of the least of these my brethren, ye have done it unto me.**

41 Then shall he say also unto them on the left hand, **Depart from me, ye cursed, into everlasting fire, prepared for the devil and his angels:**

42 **For I was an hungred, and ye gave me no meat: I was thirsty, and ye gave me no drink:**

43 **I was a stranger, and ye took me not in: naked, and ye clothed me not: sick, and in prison, and ye visited me not.**

44 Then shall they also answer him, saying, Lord, when saw we thee an hungred, or athirst, or a stranger, or naked, or sick, or in prison, and did not minister unto thee?

45 Then shall he answer them, saying, **Verily I say unto you, Inasmuch as ye did it not to one of the least of these, ye did it not to me.**

46 And these shall go away into everlasting punishment: but the righteous into life eternal.

What would Jesus do?

Jesus would feed the hungry. He would give drink to the thirsty. He would clothe the naked. He would visit the sick. He would visit those in prison. He would minister to those in need.

In the name of Jesus Christ, Amen.

9 "That was not supposed to happen!"

His sermon ended, Bishop Bruce James felt satisfied. His feelings bordered on what some might call smug euphoria. He was having trouble keeping in check his tendency to pride.
He had delivered a fine medium-length but still short talk. Just right for this hot chapel.

Constance, who was his best barometer, was smiling, which means she approved. Whenever Constance frowned and looked down or looked away, he knew he had not done well. Bishop James was grateful. Her smile was lighting up the room.

Yet there was a commotion in the back of the chapel. A person was standing, taking a haltingly long time coming toward the front. This was not supposed to happen. It was distinctly out of character with the tenor of the sacrament meeting. Everyone knew the hymn came right after the sermon. They were scheduled to sing "A Mighty Fortress Is Our God," and a benediction was needed.

As she got nearer to the front of the chapel, Bishop James recognized her. It was Mary, the young woman who had come to his doorstep. She was wearing the same clothes she had on yesterday. She struggled to climb the few stairs. All of the men including Bishop James were so stunned not one of them stood to help her. She crossed to the podium where she held onto the microphone. Better said, she half stumbled into the podium and grabbed onto the microphone to break her fall. All eyes in the congregation riveted on her.

Was she going to give a speech? Was she going to cause more disruption than she already had caused? Besides, the chapel was extremely hot and stifling and getting hotter by the minute.

The bishop worried about what to do.

Mary held onto the microphone. She leaned against the podium to keep from falling. She caught her labored breath. One could see she was arranging her thoughts. Looking from person to person. Somehow, it didn't seem right to interrupt her.

"My name is Mary Thomas," she began.

10 If "What would Jesus do?" is the second question, what is the first question?

"I was born back east. I have a Master of Divinity Degree. And I want you to know I am not drunk or high on drugs. I am stone cold sober. And I am not lying. And I am very sick. The cardiologist I saw two weeks ago told me then he thought I had but a short time to live.

"I want Bishop James to know I enjoyed his sermon today. Although, when he asked the question "What would Jesus do?" he asked only one of the right questions. It is good to ask the question "What would Jesus do?" every day of our lives. This question has come to have a primary effect of focusing the minds of most Christians on helping others. In asking "What would Jesus do?" Bishop James asked the second question.

"We must be courageous and ask the first question. As I said, the answer to the second question "What would Jesus do?" has come to mean to help the poor and the needy, to give community service, to be more charitable and kind to one another, to forebear in stressful situations, to do more good, to set up welfare centers like your Welfare Square where your good bishop sent me.

"As the bishop pointed out, the answer to this second question "What would Jesus do?" has come to be encapsulated in Matthew 25; so once more to make my point, over the years, the answer to the second question "What would Jesus do?" among us modern Christians, has come to mean "visit those who are sick and in prison and feed the hungry and clothe the naked." And all this of course is very important for all who hope to be sheep and thus found on Christ's right hand when He comes.

"There is the first question, though.

11 The first question is?

"The first question is "Would Jesus Christ Do That?" said Mary.

"This question "Would Jesus Do That?" focuses the mind on the word NO and on the word YES. It focuses the mind on standards and limits and commandments and obedience and our own sinful or righteous ways.

"For example, I have done drugs for many years. Would Jesus do marijuana? Would He do meth? Would He do cocaine? Would He do heroine? Would He sell drugs?

"I have been promiscuous for many years. Would Jesus be promiscuous? Would He sleep with his neighbor's wife? Would He sleep with someone out of wedlock? Would He be immoral in thought or deed? Would He be immoral in any way?

"I stole to support my habit. In my short lifetime I have been dishonest with myself and others. Would Jesus steal or be dishonest? Would He be dishonest and commit fraud like the corporate CEOs and officers and directors and politicians we read about or watch on television?

"I did and still do alcohol. If Jesus were here with us would He sell or addict Himself to alcohol? I smoke. Would He smoke or sell cancer tobacco?

"I have watched terrible horror and sex and violence filled movies. As a consequence of my alcohol and drug addictions, I have watched porn movies on and off the Internet. Would He do that? Would He make violent, sex-filled movies? Would He sell his soul to the devil for R and other Adult-rated big bucks? Today most if not all PG-13 movies are laced with sex and violence and foul language. Would He do that? Many Hollywood and other movie and TV writers and producers do just that. They sell their souls to the devil for money. Would Jesus do that? .

"Would Jesus bully or abuse his wife or his teenagers or little children? Would He abuse the elderly? Would He abuse His friends or neighbors or family?

"Would He gossip, tear down, and destroy His friend's or His neighbor's reputation?

Would He lie or cheat on His exams or resume? Would He shoot or blow up innocent civilians and commit terrorist acts?

"I have broken the Sabbath for many years. Would He break the Sabbath? Would He stay home from church? Would He leave his Bible on the shelf all week? Would He forget to pray and worship Our Heavenly Father? (3)

"Would He sponsor or broadcast soccer or baseball or football or basketball or golf or other sports or entertainment events on the Sabbath? Would He attend them on the Sabbath? Would He watch them on the Sabbath? Would He do that?

Would He entice and entrap our young people by advertising beer and wine with sex images during the Super bowl?

Would He buy stuff at the store on Sunday so owners and clerks of grocery and other stores would be tempted or feel compelled to stay open and violate the Sabbath?

"If Jesus Christ were here right now, it would be a different world, I assure you.

"Brothers and sisters, the first question is "Would Jesus Do That?" This first question makes us face and deal squarely with the Ten Commandments not the Ten Preferences. This first question makes us address and follow the highest standards of ethics, morality and goodness. I have learned too late in my life that without standards of righteousness, helping the poor and the needy is fine but more often than not lacks common virtue.

"The first question "Would Jesus Christ do that?" is a preventive question. It provides a fence at the top of the cliff. By living up to Christ's standards of morality and righteousness there naturally are fewer sinners and poor and needy to help.

The second question "What would Jesus do?" focuses on deploying the ambulances down in the valley.

Asking "Would Jesus do that?" prevents problems at the top of the cliff. Asking "What would Jesus do?" has come to mean giving Christian service by helping to fix the problems after the fact down at the bottom of the cliff.

12 Mary Thomas

"So Brothers and sisters, I was Mary Thomas the alcoholic. I was Mary Thomas the meth addict. I was Mary Thomas the chain smoker. I was Mary Thomas the promiscuous. I was Mary Thomas the thief and liar.

"I am also Mary Thomas holder of a divinity degree. I am Mary Thomas the once beautiful woman. I am Mary Thomas wearing baggy, worn out Levis, a threadbare shirt and a red stained sweater. I am still Mary Thomas, a child of God.

Discomfort from lack of air conditioning was not what was discomforting those in the congregation. Mary's words were burning right through each heart.

Then she collapsed, barely holding onto and laying her head on the podium.

Doctor Anderson, who had been sitting with his family near the front of the chapel, was one of the first at her side. He listened to her heart with his stethoscope. "I am afraid she told the truth. She is a very sick woman.

Mary Thomas whispered into the microphone and all could hear her last simple words. "Fix it, Bishop James, Fix it! Would Jesus Christ do that? Then Mary Thomas closed her eyes.

13 Would He do that?

The paramedics took Mary Thomas to St. Marks Hospital. But the doctors could not help her. Mary did not wake up. She stayed in a coma and died several days later.

Bishop James conducted a simple graveside service. A wooden casket. A pauper's grave. No family present. A number from the ward attended.

"A pauper's casket and a pauper's grave," said Bishop James quietly. "Yet, for all of that, Mary's words and influence will not be forgotten."

Each Sunday Brother Swenson taped the sacrament meeting talks. He taped Mary's sermon as well.

As part of the short graveside service, Bishop James placed a copy of what may well have been Mary's first and last sermon on her casket. Brother Swenson had typed a cover page which simply read: "Would Jesus Christ Do That?"

After the service, Bruce quietly said to Constance, "I think I will walk home if you don't mind driving the car."

Ever obliging, Constance drove the car home. Bishop Bruce James walked home alone. Head down. Pondering. Praying. Wondering.

14 The Bishop thought: Would Jesus break the Ten Commandments?

Would He do that? Bishop James mentally ticked off the Ten Commandments in his mind.

1 Would He worship other gods?

2 Would He make graven images of money and glittering clothing and multi-million dollar show houses and cars and boats and stock and money and other things of this world and actually or in effect worship them?

3 Would He take the name of God His Father in vain? Would He swear or use the name of God in vain as an expletive?

4 Would He desecrate and break the Sabbath? Would He turn the Sabbath into a day of work or recreation, or football and soccer and basketball and golf and tennis and equestrian events and television entertainment all for money or prestige or love of sports and entertainment?

5 Would He dishonor His father or mother? Would He avoid taking care of His aged parents?

6 Would He kill or do anything like unto it? Would he murder? Would he abort millions of babies every year?

7 Would He fornicate or commit adultery or do anything like unto it including selling and indulging annually in billions of dollars of pornography?

8 Would He steal or do anything like unto it including burglary or corporate CEO and officer and director and politician fraud?

9 Would He bear false witness or lie or do anything like unto it including tearing down another person's reputation for political or personal gain?

10 Would He covet his neighbor's wife or husband or children or car or house or job or income? Would He covet and take money at the expense of the environment or His integrity?

No, He would not do any of those things!

15 Would He do drugs? Bishop James thought.

Bruce had read before that on occasion "Jesus wept." During his walk home, Bruce James, Salt Lake City inner-city bishop, thought about the terrible problems in his ward and community and Bruce felt tears running down his cheeks. He was dealing with 50 welfare situations at the moment and he had few volunteers to help him and he was emotionally and physically overwhelmed.

Would Jesus do marijuana? Methamphetamines? Cocaine? Heroin? Abuse oxycodone and other prescription drugs? Would He addict himself to tobacco and alcohol and pornography? So many of the most serious problems in the inner-city were caused by these terrible addictions.

16 Would Jesus keep His Father's commandments while proactively helping others?

"Would He keep His Father's commandments?

"Would He uphold and live according to the laws of the land?

"Would He proactively help others?

"Would He protect little children?

"Would He help teenagers through boy scout and other youth activities?

"Would He protect and help the elderly?

"Would He visit and help those in prison?

"Would He help the poor and the needy?

"Would He feed the hungry?

"Would He visit and help the sick?

"Would He love his family?

Bishop James knew the answer to each of these questions. He knew what he had to do. He would focus much more of his work on answering Mary Thomas' "first" question.

17 Bishop James' first talk after Mary's passing. Would Jesus worship other gods?

"Well, folks, another Sunday has come and I have decided to take a few minutes in Sunday School and talk to you." The bishop straightened some papers and his scriptures on the podium. "Thank goodness the building air conditioner is back working. In light of my sobering experience with Mary Thomas including her graveside service, I want to invite your participation and have a discussion.

"I want to use Mary Thomas's question. I want to ask you "Would Jesus do that?" and to begin I want to use the Ten Commandments as my frame of reference.

"Mary told us something simple yet complex and profound. Mary told us if Jesus Christ would not do it we ought not do it either.

"I know it may appear to be impossible for us mere mortals to determine what a God would do. And He is God as is Our Father in Heaven.

"Notwithstanding, it is possible to study God's word and to determine what Jesus would do because Jesus took the time to tell us and even model for us specifically what He would do. He set the great example. He showed us the way to happiness and peace.

"And so today, not as a point of departure, but rather as a point of new beginning, and in the spirit of Mary Thomas' sermon, and from God's Ten Commandments, I ask you these three simple questions keying off of the first and the second and the third of the Ten Commandments: "Would Jesus worship other gods? Would He make graven images and worship them? Would He take the name of God in vain? Would He do that?

Nancy Carter, the young wife of Andy Carter, was first to raise her hand. "No, Bishop. He would not do that." Jesus was a man of prayer, sometimes rising long before daybreak to find a secluded place and pray, sometimes praying all night. He was a man of worship, always finding time to worship His Father; always honoring His Father.

"That is right," Nancy. "Let's read a couple of scriptures."

"In Deuteronomy 10 verse 12 we read: "Serve the Lord thy God with all thy heart" and in 1 Chronicles 16 verse 19 we read "Worship the Lord in the beauty of his holiness.""

"In Psalm 81 verse 9 we read: "Neither shalt thou worship any strange god." And in Isaiah chapter 2 verses 7 through 8 we read, and this I think prophetically applies particularly to our day: "Their land also is full of silver and gold, neither is there any end of their treasures; their land is also full of horses, neither is there any end of their chariots: Their land also is full of idols; they worship the work of their own hands, that which their own fingers have made.""

"How are these verses from Isaiah applicable to our day, Nancy?

Nancy said. "Bishop, our land is full of untold wealth. Our land is full of endless treasures. In our land there is no end to the number of our "chariot" automobiles. Our land is full of things to buy and it is not a far stretch of the imagination to accuse our society of worshiping the work of our own hands, of worshiping cars and clothes and money and art and sex and the sexual and violent images on television and in other media. Our land is filled with television idols if you define our television sets as idols," replied Nancy. There is even a television show called American Idol.'"

A nervous twitter of laughter could be heard throughout the room.

Bishop James read another passage: "In Isaiah 53 verse 6 we read: "All we like sheep have gone astray; we have turned every one to his own way; …" The word "All" is all inclusive. All we like sheep have gone astray; we have turned away from worshiping God to worshiping money. We keep working to get ahead of our neighbors.

"The word *worship* is a fascinating word. It means the ardent, reverent love or devotion or honor or esteem accorded a deity, idol, or object. It means participation in religious rites.

"Would Jesus honor and esteem a deity other than His Father in Heaven? No, He would not. Would He honor and esteem and devote his life to money and things and the prevalent evil television programming and pornographic movies? No, He would not. Would He employ his time on the Sabbath attending Church and worshiping God in spirit and truth, in sacrament and prayer? Would He spend his time on the Sabbath with his family and helping those in need? Yes, He would.

"Taking the name of God in vain is a painful subject to me. I hear it everywhere. I hear it in television shows and movies. I hear it at the grocery store. I hear it in restaurants. I heard it when I worked at the office. And I hear it once in a while even in the Church building and especially at basketball and football and soccer games. I will substitute the word "blank" for the name of God the Father or Jesus. I hear adults and teenagers and children saying: "Oh, blank." I hear "blank" used as an expletive. I hear "blank" used for emphasis. I hear "blank" used as punctuation. It is not right! It is a grievous sin to use the name of deity lightly. It is sinful to use the name of God in vain. God will not hold us guiltless if we take His name in vain. Would Jesus do that? He of all persons would not take the name of God in vain.

"So, Nancy, as conclusion: Jesus Christ worshiped His Father. He did not worship other gods including money or cars or clothes or jewelry or television shows or movies or actors or pornography. He did not take the name of his Father in vain. We should not do so either.

"Think about these three commandments this week. And ask yourself, if Jesus were here, Would He do that?

18 Would He break the Sabbath?

"I hope you had an excellent week. For my lesson this week, I would like to focus on keeping the Sabbath day holy. And once again I would like to deliver my lesson in the spirit of Mary Thomas' question Would Jesus do that?

"Millions of Americans and millions of people in other countries break the Sabbath each week.

"Millions attend, watch or participate in NFL football, or world cup soccer, or NCAA basketball, or PGA golf, or concerts, or other sporting or entertainment events that are held on the Sabbath.

"Millions spend their Sabbath days hiking, mountain climbing, camping, boating, fishing, hunting, and car racing, traveling, gambling, or watching pornography on the Internet.

"Throughout the Old Testament, God and His prophets have commanded His people to keep the Sabbath day holy. I have asked Todd Harris to read from the Ten Commandments and another scripture which deals with keeping the Sabbath day holy. I have also asked Todd to read the story of a man who broke the Sabbath by gathering sticks, and the penalty God imposed upon this man for doing so.

Todd Harris: I am reading from Exodus 20 verses 8 through 11. "Remember the Sabbath day, to keep it holy. Six days shalt thou labour, and do all thy work: But the seventh day is the Sabbath of the LORD thy God: in it thou shalt not do any work, thou, nor thy son, nor thy daughter, thy manservant, nor thy maidservant, nor thy cattle, nor thy stranger that is within thy gates: For in six days the LORD made heaven and earth, the sea, and all that in them is, and rested the seventh day: wherefore the LORD blessed the Sabbath day, and hallowed it."

"From Exodus 31:12 thru 17: "And the LORD spake unto Moses saying, Speak thou also unto the children of Israel, saying, Verily my Sabbaths ye shall keep: for it is a sign between me and you throughout your generations; that ye may know that I am the LORD that doth sanctify you. Ye shall keep the Sabbath therefore; for it is holy unto you: every one that defileth it shall surely be put to death: for whosoever doeth any work therein, that soul shall be cut off from among his people. Six days may work be done; but in the seventh is the Sabbath of rest, holy to the LORD: whosoever doeth any work in the Sabbath day, he shall surely be put to death. Wherefore the children of Israel shall keep the Sabbath, to observe the Sabbath throughout their generations, for a perpetual covenant. It is a sign between me and the children of Israel for ever: for in six days the LORD made heaven and earth, and on the seventh day he rested, and was refreshed.""

"The bible story Bishop James asked me to read is from the book of Numbers verses 32 thru 36. "And while the children of Israel were in the wilderness, they found a man that gathered sticks upon the Sabbath day. And they that found him gathering sticks brought him unto Moses and Aaron, and unto the entire congregation. And they put him in ward, because it was not declared what should be done to him. And the LORD said unto Moses, The man shall be surely put to death: the entire congregation shall stone him with stones without the camp. And the entire congregation brought him without the camp, and stoned him with stones, and he died; as the LORD commanded Moses.""

"Thank you Todd," said Bishop James. "Now let's turn to the New Testament. Todd, please read Matthew chapter 12 verses 1 thru 13."

Todd: "At that time Jesus went on the Sabbath day through the corn; and his disciples were an hungred, and began to pluck the ears of corn, and to eat. But when the Pharisees saw it, they said unto him, Behold, thy disciples do that which is not lawful to do upon the Sabbath day. But he said unto them, **Have ye not read what David did, when he was an hungred, and they that were with him; How he entered into the house of God, and did eat the showbread, which was not lawful for him to eat, neither for them which were with him, but only for the priests? Or have ye not read in the law, how that on the Sabbath days the priests in the temple profane the Sabbath, and are blameless? But I say unto you, That in this place is one greater than the temple. But if ye had known what this meaneth, I will have mercy, and not sacrifice, ye would not have condemned the guiltless. For the Son of man is Lord even of the Sabbath day.** And when he was departed thence, he went into their synagogue: And, behold, there was a man which had his hand withered. And they asked him, saying, Is it lawful to heal on the Sabbath days? that they might accuse him. And he said unto them, **What man shall there be among you, that shall have one sheep, and if it fall into a pit on the Sabbath day, will he not lay hold on it, and lift it out? How much then is a man better than a sheep? Wherefore it is lawful to do well on the Sabbath days.** Then saith he to the man, **Stretch forth thine hand,** And he stretched it forth; and it was restored whole, like as the other.""

"Thank you," said Bishop James. "Todd, what principles do we find in these passages?"

Todd: "Bishop, from these scriptures we conclude that God is deadly serious in his expectation that we honor the Sabbath day and keep it holy; that we treat it as a day of rest. Though in our day we are not stoned and we don't lose our lives when we work on the Sabbath, it is fair to say that we lose some fraction of our spiritual lives when we work and do business and sports and entertainment on the Sabbath. It is acceptable to take care of the need for food. It is acceptable to God that we do good on the Sabbath. Obviously, community services have to be maintained like fire, police, medical, and military. There is little excuse for working or engaging in sports on the Sabbath."

"Thank you again, Todd," said Bishop James. "The Sabbath is a day of rest. More importantly, the Sabbath is a holy day. The Sabbath is a holy day in which we are to turn our whole souls to God. It is a day of prayer and worship, a day in which we can attend our Church meetings and listen to the word of God, a day when we can spend quiet time with our families. Sabbath day observance is one of our greatest tests. It separates a righteous person from a worldly and even wicked person. It is a day in which no unnecessary work should be done. There are six other days for recreation, sports, hunting, fishing, entertainment, travel, and shopping. The Sabbath is a day of worship. God rested on the Sabbath after His labors in creating the earth and he asks the same of us. Would Jesus keep the Sabbath day holy? Certainly, He would.

Todd: "Bishop, I know this question is coming at you out of left field, and probably doesn't have much to do with your words about the Sabbath, but I've been wondering if there is a description of the Savior anywhere in the scriptures?

Bishop James: "You know, Todd, I'm glad you asked. And your question is in fact related. In John's writing in his New Testament Book of Revelation, Chapter 1, we first read about Christ's Second Coming, and then we read an account of John's experience when John actually saw the Savior on "the Lord's day."

7 Behold, he cometh with clouds; and every eye shall see him, and they also which pierced him: and all kindreds of the earth shall wail because of him. Even so, Amen.

8 I am Alpha and Omega, the beginning and the ending, saith the Lord, which is, and which was, and which is to come, the Almighty.

9 I John, who also am your brother, and companion in tribulation, and in the kingdom and patience of Jesus Christ, was in the isle that is called Patmos, for the word of God, and for the testimony of Jesus Christ.

10 I was in the Spirit on the Lord's day, and heard behind me a great voice, as of a trumpet,

11 Saying, I am Alpha and Omega, the first and the last: and, What thou seest, write in a book, ...

12 And I turned to see the voice that spake with me. And being turned, I saw seven golden candlesticks;

13 And in the midst of the seven candlesticks one like unto the Son of man, clothed with a garment down to the foot, and girt about the paps with a golden girdle.

14 His head and his hairs were white like wool, as white as snow; and his eyes were as a flame of fire;

15 And his feet like unto fine brass, as if they burned in a furnace; and his voice as the sound of many waters.

16 And he had in his right hand seven stars: and out of his mouth went a sharp two edged sword: and his countenance was as the sun shineth in his strength.

17 And when I saw him, I fell at his feet as dead. And he laid his right hand upon me, saying unto me, Fear not; I am the first and the last:

18 I am he that liveth, and was dead; and, behold, I am alive for evermore, Amen; and have the keys of hell and of death.

19 The Bishop's interview with Andy. Would Jesus care for His parents?

The young man was seventeen. He and his family were long time friends. The boy's breath and person smelled of stale tobacco with a touch of liquor. Bishop James offered him some mints which he grabbed at.

"You haven't been to see your mother for a long time, have you, Andy?"

The young man dropped his gaze to the floor. "No, Bishop."

"Why not, Andy?"

I haven't felt like it," said Andy.

"Why not?" Bishop James pressed.

"It makes me uncomfortable to be in the house with her."

"Have you figured out why?"

Andy paused for some time before speaking in low tones. "It's probably because I am doing some things she doesn't approve of."

"Would Jesus do those things your mother disapproves of, Andy? Would He do that?"

"No, Bishop, he would not."

"Do you think your mother loves you greatly and only wants the best for you?"

"Yes."

"What are you going to do about it?"

"I'll go and see her right now, Bishop."

"Is that a promise?"

"Yes."

"Do you know what it means to honor your father and mother, Andy?"

"I think so, Bishop. It means to make them proud by doing those things that are right."

The Bishop smiled. "Good answer, Andy. It also means visiting them, calling them on the phone, helping them do their chores as they age and need physical help. Now go and make those visits happen, Andy."

Andy smiled. "I will Bishop. I'll start today.

"Andy, here is a pocket-size copy of the New Testament and a short handout so you can become better acquainted with Jesus. Last year, we studied the Book of Mormon. This year we are studying the New Testament in Sunday School and I am giving this pocket-size New Testament to each person I interview. Please read the Gospel of John and my handout, will you?"

Andy hesitated but took the little book and the handout.

20 The Bishop interviews Tom and Edith. Would Jesus report child abuse?

The bishop's second interview was with a young couple, Tom and Edith Travis. They had a three-year-old little girl Jody and a four-year-old little boy Amos in preschool and the manager of the pre-school had spanked the little children very hard when they were, according to her way of thinking, "naughty." There was more than a hint there might have been sexual abuse. Todd and Edith had come seeking Bishop James' advice.

"Child abuse is a horrible thing," muttered the bishop as he rummaged through papers to find a phone number on his desk. "I have this community hotline I will dial and you must report the abuse and launch an investigation.

The bishop continued: "Tom and Edith, protecting and healing our abused and neglected children is a priority for all of us. Educating families about the evils of child-abuse and how to cope with it is critical. Would Jesus abuse a little child? Of course not! In fact, Jesus was emphatic. Of child abuse, he said: **"Whoso shall offend one of these little ones which believe in me, it were better for him that a millstone were hanged about his neck, and that he were drowned in the depth**

of the sea." (Matthew 18:6) We are to protect our children. We are duty bound to strengthen the family. We must provide a home and a community environment of love and support. It is my duty to report child abuse. It is your duty to do the same. It is your duty as parents to take aggressive action to protect your little children. How are they doing and what can we do to help them?

"They are at our home with my mother," Edith replied.

Bishop James was just getting warmed up. "Little children are easily victims because they cannot protect themselves. Helping and protecting them must be a first and primary concern. There is zero tolerance for the perpetrators of any form of child abuse. We can try to help the perpetrator, but we cannot and will not tolerate child abuse in any form. I know there are some who cite clergy privilege when information about child abuse is obtained during a confession; but there is in fact absolutely no clergy privilege when it comes to confession and child abuse. We must report it and focus on helping and protecting the children we know and and others who may be in the grasp of child abusers.

"Also, Tom and Edith, here are two small pocket size copies of the New Testament and a short handout. I would like you to become better acquainted with our Savior by reading my handout and my favorite gospel which is the Gospel of John. Will you do that?"

21 Bishop James' visit with Jack and Janet. Would Jesus be kind to His wife?

The bishop's last visit of the day was with a middle-age couple, Jack and Janet Thompson. The two of them had come to him for marital counseling. Janet complained of Jack's insensitivity and verbal abuse. Jack complained of Janet's incessant criticism and verbal abuse. Bishop James listened intently for more than forty five minutes as each told his and her tale of woe and heartache.

Then Bishop James interrupted: "You know, Janet and Jack, this is our third session and to-date all I have done is listen to you two complain about each other. I think it is now my turn to comment. Would you agree?

Jack and Janet nodded grudgingly.

"Would Jesus do that?" the bishop asked. Would He complain and find fault with and criticize his spouse? Would He be insensitive to the needs of his wife? I don't think so. My conclusion is, after listening to both of you for a long time, you don't need me as your counselor. You don't need a bishop to sit for three hours and listen to you complain. All you need to do is what Jesus would do. He treated others with love and kindness. So treat each other with love and kindness. So now I am going to ask you to promise God the following. I ask each of you to promise God that next time you have any inclination to criticize or find fault or be unkind or insensitive, you will ask the question "Would Jesus do that? " Please raise your hand" as indication you have made that promise."

Jack and Janet each raised a hand.

"Next, I want you to promise you will ask a second question "What would Jesus do?" Please raise your hand again as indication you have made and will keep that promise.

Jack and Janet each raised a hand.

"Now, promise me that you will do what you think Jesus would do.

Jack and Janet each raised a hand automatically.

"Take this as an assignment for the next month until we meet again to review your progress. I will have Constance make an appointment so we can meet one month from today at the same time. And thank you for coming. And thank you for making such important promises. You won't be sorry you did."

"Also, Jack and Janet, here are two small pocket size copies of the New Testament and a short handout. Especially take time to read my favorite gospel which is the Gospel of John. Will you do that?

They each smiled and again raised a hand.

22 Bruce and Constance. Would Jesus support abortion?

They started many years ago reading out loud from a book each night just before they said their prayers. Their diligence had brought them many happy hours of reading, discussion and learning. They read the Old Testament several times out loud. They also read the New Testament out loud several times. They read commentaries on the Bible. They read commentaries on the The Dead Sea Scrolls. They read the Apocrypha. The read The Book of Mormon several times. They read historical and biographical works about Abraham Lincoln, Thomas Jefferson, John Adams, and other famous people. They read a number of the classics. Constance read out loud on even days. Bruce read out loud on his odd days.

They had taken a detour from religious and historical and biographical works and were reading a "Crime Clock from The Department of Justice":

"Every 23.1 seconds there is one violent crime.
"Every 32.6 minutes there is one murder.
"Every 5.6 minutes there is a forcible rape.

"Every 1.3 minutes there is one robbery.
"Every 36.9 seconds there is an aggravated assault.
"Every 3.1 seconds there is one property crime.
"Every 14.7 seconds there is one burglary.
"Every 4.5 seconds there is one larceny-theft.
"Every 25.5 seconds there is one motor vehicle theft.

"This Crime Clock should be viewed with care. It conveys the annual reported crime experience by showing a relative frequency of occurrence of certain offenses. It should not be taken to imply any regularity in the commission of crime.

"The Crime Clock represents the annual ratio of crime to fixed time intervals."

"Whatever that means," Constance said as she continued:

"Violent crime is composed of four offenses: murder and non negligent manslaughter, forcible rape, robbery, and aggravated assault.

"According to the Uniform Crime Reporting (UCR) Program's definition, violent crimes involve force or threat of force.

"In 2004 there were 1,367,009 offenses which represented 465.5 per 100,000 inhabitants.

"Of the 1,367,009 violent crimes nationwide, aggravated assaults comprised 62.5 percent, robbery 29.4 percent, forcible rape 6.9 percent, and murder 1.2 percent.

"In terms of the rate of offenses for each of the four violent crimes, aggravated assault had the highest rate, estimated at 291.1 offenses per 100,000 inhabitants.

"There were an estimated 136.7 robberies, 32.2 forcible rapes, and 5.5 murders for each 100,000 resident population in 2004."

Constance then read the number of legal abortions performed in the United States.

"Depending on which group you accept, the Centers for Disease Control or the Alan Guttmacher Institute, it states that in 1973 there were between 615,831 and 744,600.
"In 2001 there were between 853,485 and 1,303,000 abortions.
"Each year in between was similar.
"The number for 2004 was 1,293,000.
"In 1994 60.5 percent were white, 34.7 percent were black, and 4.8 percent were other.
"Approximately 46,000,000 abortions are performed annually worldwide.

"That is about 126,000 babies killed per day and I don't believe those numbers include illegal abortions. Would Jesus kill or do anything like unto it?" Constance quietly said. "Would He kill the unborn? If Jesus were here, would He hurt and kill others and especially babies? Would He do that? "

Bruce was quiet for a few moments. "In Second Kings Chapters 16 and 17 and 21 we read that in ancient times, the children of Israel killed their sons and their daughters by causing them to pass through the fire as part of the parents' worship of the God Molech. In Leviticus 18 God commanded his people not to do that but they didn't listen to him and stop that evil practice. In return for their terrible sin of killing their children, in Ezekiel 16 we read that God diminished their ordinary food and delivered them unto the will of those who hated them and caused them to be thrust through with the sword and caused their houses to be burned with fire.

Today, we have a similar situation where millions of unborn children are caused to pass to their death through the fire of abortion. I do believe that the people of this world are in for a monumental surprise. Jesus loves the innocent child and the repentant righteous adult. In the millennial prophecy found in Isaiah 11 verse 4 we read that He intends to slay the wicked with the breath of His mouth when he comes in His great power and glory in a few years to usher in his great millennial reign on earth. I tremble when I read Isaiah 11 verse 4. Jesus is not pleased with the wicked and when He comes they will receive their comeuppance of immense and painful proportion. And I cannot but believe that those who countenance abortions will be classed among the wicked when he comes.

23 Another Sunday talk. Would Jesus be immoral?

Bishop James stood at the podium delivering a tough Ten Commandments sermon to his congregation.

"Adultery is a horrible sin for it destroys family relationships. Fornication is equivalent horrible sin because it does the same thing. "Thou shalt not commit adultery," is one of the Ten Commandments in Exodus 20 verse 14. Sex immorality is next to murder in the category of personal sins. Anciently the penalty for adultery or fornication was death. "The adulterer and the adulteress shall surely be put to death," we read in Leviticus chapter 20 verse 10 and Deuteronomy chapter 22 verses 21 and 29. In Malachi chapter 3 verse 5 and Malachi chapter 4 verse 1 we read at the Lord's Second Coming, He will be a swift witness against adulterers and they will be burned as stubble and cast down to hell. Adultery and fornication are springboards to divorce, illegitimacy, violence, broken homes, and physical disease.

"Adultery and fornication are created first out of lust in the mind according to Matthew 15 verse 19 and the same is true of any other immoral act. Would Jesus commit adultery or do anything like unto it? No, he would not. Some adultery and fornication and other sexual immorality is easily traced back to child sex abuse and sex laden television shows and movies and to pornography addiction.

"Would Jesus use pornography and watch movies or television with sex content? Would He do that?

"Let me share with you some statistics Constance read me the other evening. Did you know that two in five Internet users visited an adult site in August of 2005 according to tracking by comScore Media Metrix. Did you know that 87% of university students polled have virtual sex via internet pornography? Did you know that there were 63.4 million unique visitors to adult websites in December 2005, reaching 37.2% of the internet audience. Did you also know that 20 U.S. companies accounted for more than 70% of 297 million porn links on the Internet. Did you know that by the end of 2004, there were 420 million pages of pornography and that the industry generates more than $12 billion dollars annually. Did you know that the largest group of viewers of internet porn is children between ages of 12 and 17.

"Did you know that according to comScore Media Metrix, Internet users viewed over 15 billion pages of adult pornography content in August of 2005. Did you know that according to comScore Media Metrix, Internet users spent an average of 14.6 minutes per day viewing adult content online. Did you know that more than 32 million unique individuals visited a porn site in the month of September of 2003 alone and that nearly 22.8 million were male (71 percent) while 9.4 million adult site visitors were female (29%). And did you know that 25% of porn sites mousetrap a viewer thus not permitting him or her to exit the site once he or she has entered.

"Well, what should and can be done about it?

"If any of what I have said applies to you, begin with yourself and repent by changing your ways and cleaning up your thoughts and your acts and receiving the forgiveness that comes by Christ's atonement.

"The best medicine, antidote and cure, is Jesus and his gospel of righteousness and peace. A corollary best medicine is discipline to avoid all pornography and sexually and violence explicit media.

My seven step seven day recovery program may help you if you are troubled by pornography or sex sin.

Step 1. Day1. Without any reservation, accept complete responsibility for your sin.

Step 2. Day 2. Pray to the Father in the name of Jesus Christ, and confess the exact nature of your sin.

Step 3. Day 3. Promise God you will not indulge that sin again.

Step 4. Day 4. Block pornographic Internet sites or TV channels and destroy all pornography.

Step 5. Day 5. Accept Christ's Atonement, his suffering for your sins in Gethsemane and on the cross, repent, change your ways, and courageously keep God's commandments.

Step 6. Day 6. Pledge out loud that you will not do pornography.

Step 7. Day 7. Take one of these steps each day until your temptation to sin is eradicated.

In conclusion, love your wife or husband with all of your heart, and cleave unto her or him and unto none else. And if you need counseling, call me. I can help you and I also have the names and phone numbers of several good family services counselors.

24 Would Jesus steal or bear false witness or covet?

"The eighth commandment is "Thou shalt not steal." Yet, as I mentioned in one of my earlier talks, and depending on how one looks at the statistics, every 1.3 minutes in the United States there is one robbery – someone forcibly stealing something from someone else. There were 106.7 robberies per 100,000 population. Every 14.7 seconds there is a burglary in the United States. Every 4.5 seconds there is one larceny theft in the U.S. Every 25.5 seconds there is one motor vehicle theft.

"The ninth commandment is "Thou shalt not bear false witness" which is one way of saying "Thou shalt not lie or commit perjury or fraud." In the media, we continue to encounter stories of corporate greed wherein CEOs are convicted of corporate fraud and insider trading. As well, the sheer volume of lying by and about political candidates or other public figures is staggering. The junk media tabloids and the legitimate press rip the envelope when it comes to sensationalism. Lying and gossip and innuendo and slander are rampant in the media and especially in the political arena, but they are also epidemic in our families, neighborhoods, homes, and churches. Would Jesus do that? He would not.

"The tenth commandment is "Thou shalt not covet." Yet thousands of get rich quick schemes abound on the Internet and in magazines and on cable television and in businesses throughout the nation. We are a nation of debtors and the debt loads are staggering, much of which debt is incurred because people covet more stuff or get involved in get rich quick schemes. To covet is to feel an unrighteous desire for something that is possessed by another. To covet is to feel an unrighteous desire for that which belongs to another. To covet is to wish, long, or crave for something, and usually property, that belongs to another person. To covet is to be envious of another person. To covet is to begrudge the fact that someone else has something. The sin of covetousness is also manifest in a special way. It is manifest especially in the great sin of gambling.

"God not only wants us to avoid certain actions, but also he wants us to avoid certain misdirected thoughts, not the least of which is inordinate desire for our neighbor's house, wife, servants, money, or other property including no doubt his riding lawn mower. It is intriguing that the commandment not to covet is the tenth commandment, and God has commanded his children not to covet their own property but rather to tithe of their increase and give a tenth into his storehouse according to the commandment that is found in the book of Malachi. Rabbi Arnold Jacob Wolf, in "*Broken Tablets*," a Jewish Lights Publishing book, continues to write: 'It is not forbidden to wish to have a house like my neighbor's house or a car like his or even a woman just like his wife. What is forbidden … is to want his car or his wife, her house or her husband … It is all right to want to have a big house. It is forbidden to want to live in someone else's house or life. I am commanded to be me, not you or her. I am forbidden to covet your place, to wish to be you.' Rabbi Rachel S. Mikva in the same "*Broken Tablets*" writes: 'to covet is to deny our own life and our own being, which God cannot abide.' To covet is to desire deeply a relationship with material or other things or people other than God. To covet is to buy things and accumulate things at the expense of faith in and service to God. To covet is to engage in idolatry or false worship. Gratitude is an opposite of covetousness."

Bishop James continued. "In closing, I want to say something about the sin of gambling. There is gambling and then there is pathological gambling. Both are wrong. A person is a pathological gambler if he or she is preoccupied with past, future, present, or fantasy gambling experiences.

"A person is a pathological gambler if he or she has developed a state of intolerance wherin he or she requires larger or more frequent bets to achieve the same "rush."

"A person is a pathological gambler if he or she has withdrawal symptoms wherein he or she gets highly restless or irritable whenever there is an attempt to stop or reduce gambling frequency or amounts.

"A person is a pathological gambler if he or she uses gambling to escape serious personal or family or financial or marriage or other problems.

"A person is a pathological gambler if he or she works overtime to win back gambling losses with more gambling, thus chasing after an earlier state of being where he or she won or had more money or property.

"A person is a pathological gambler if he or she lies to spouse or other family and friends and therapists and tries to hide the extent of gambling and gambling losses.

"A person is a pathological gambler if he or she is out of control, trying over and over and over again unsuccessfully to eliminate or reduce gambling.

"A person is a pathological gambler if he or she breaks the law, committing illegal acts to get more gambling money or to make up gambling losses.

"A person is a pathological gambler if he or she is willing to or in fact does give up a significant personal relationship or other important opportunity in order to gamble.

"A person is a pathological gambler if he or she turns to any third party for financial assistance including spouse, other family members, friends, business associates in order to bail him or her out of her gambling predicament.

"I took this detail about pathological gambling from the Internet and especially from a Wikipedia subject titled Problem Gambling.

25 Bishop James talks to the inner-city young adults about addiction? Would Jesus do meth?

"Today I don't want to talk to you about marijuana, heroin, cocaine, tobacco, alcohol, or oxycontin. These are perhaps addiction topics for another day and in any case the same principles apply. Today I want to focus on addiction to that powerful stimulant crystal meth.

"If one or more of you are or a family member is suffering from meth addiction, if there is any way I can convince you to get treatment, to go to or to get your family member to go to a detox center, I plead with you to do so.

"Methamphetamines create these short-term effects:

-- Euphoria or rush if smoked or injected.

-- This rush is believed to be caused by release of the neurotransmitter dopamine into those sections of the brain that regulate feelings of pleasure

-- A long lasting high if snorted

-- An increase in physical activity

-- A decrease in fatigue

-- An increase in attention

-- A decrease in appetite

-- An increase in respiration

-- Hyperthermia

-- Elevated body temperature

-- Convulsions

"Methamphetamines causes these long-term effects:

-- Serious dependence addiction

-- Functional and molecular changes to the brain

-- Violent behavior

-- Anxiety

-- Confusion

-- Insomnia

-- Paranoia

-- Auditory hallucinations

-- Mood disturbances

-- Delusions

-- Sensations of insects creeping on the skin (the word for this phenomenon is "formication")

-- Homicidal thoughts

-- Suicidal thoughts

-- Stroke

-- Weight loss

-- Repetitive motor activity

-- Hallucinations

-- Addiction psychosis

-- Foregoing food

-- Foregoing sleep

-- Out-of-control rages

-- Pregressive social and occupational deterioration

"Medical complications from meth use include:

-- A variety of very serious cardiovascular problems

-- Irreversible stroke-producing damage to small blood vessels in the brain

-- Rapid heart rate

-- Inflammation of the heart lining

-- Irregular heartbeat

-- Increased blood pressure

-- Enlargement of the heart

-- Thinning of the heart wall

-- Aggravation of any heart condition

-- Acute lead poisoning

-- Convulsions

-- Hypothermia which is elevated body temperature

-- Skin abscesses

-- Prenatal complications

-- Increased rates of premature delivery

-- Altered neonatal behavioral patterns such as abnormal reflexes and extreme irritability

-- Congenital deformities of the newborn

"Withdrawal from meth results in

-- Intense craving for the drug

-- Aggression

-- Paranoia

-- Fatigue

-- Anxiety

-- Depression

-- Damage to dopamine-producing and serotonin-containing brain cells

"I built this list from a number of Internet sites simply by Googling 'effects of meth.' What more need I say?

26 Bishop James' lesson to the young men in his ward and his analogy or parable of the Garbage Cans coupled with the fact that there are a great many blessings that come from keeping God's commandments!

"In my lesson today, I want to share with you what I call my parable of the garbage cans, and before I do so, I do want you to know that I am well aware of the fact that most analogies or parables break down at some point. Anyway, here goes. My parable of the garbage cans.

"I have a number of garbage cans at my house: one under the sink in the kitchen, one in each bathroom, one in Constance's home office, one in my home office. I even have a small garbage can in the garage which I use for recyclables. Several of my neighbors keep their garbage cans inside their garage so you would never know they have garbage cans unless they open their garage door. My one neighbor has his garbage cans parked right in front of his garage so there is no question whatsoever that he has garbage cans. I also have two large garbage cans standing beside my house. I try to set them back from the street so not everyone can see them although if you pay attention, you can tell they are there. Of course, I've got my garbage cans just like everybody else in the neighborhood. Anyway, in my big dark black garbage can I put my foul, smelly, ugly, dirty, trash; you know, the wet, gooey stuff I really don't want to touch. In my second big blue garbage can I put my recyclable items: you know, the newspapers, plastic bottles and other plastic items, card board boxes, some glass items. Each week I roll my big black garbage can out to the curb and once a month I roll my big blue garbage can out to the curb. And each week a huge garbage truck drives up to my house, empties my black garbage can, and hauls the trash off to the dump where it is buried or burned. And once a month, another garbage truck drives up to my house, empties my blue garbage can, and hauls the recyclables off to the sorting place at the recycling factory to undergo a refinement process. Our sins are much like mental and spiritual garbage; and these sins arise from willfully and knowingly breaking God's commandments; and the truth is each of us who is older than eight years old and who is able to think reasonably has sinned and come short of the glory of God. Notwithstanding, each week by the process of repentance and spiritual change, these sins can be dumped into the black garbage can to be sent to the dump where they can be buried or burned. Minor faults and lack of refinement and omissions as a general rule seem to be like the recyclable trash and likewise through the process of repentance and change they too can be dumped into the blue garbage can once a month to be sent to the sorting place and the recycling factory for refinement. Well, you can think about this analogy or parable and draw some of your own conclusions. It is obviously helpful if you make a concerted effort each week to dump your smelly garbage sins; as well, it is very helpful when you make a concerted effort at least once a month to get rid of your less offensive recyclables and refine your life.

"Well, enough of my parable of the garbage cans. I also want to remind each of you today, lest anyone think the gospel message is harsh or uncaring, Christ's gospel is the good news for all of us. It is the triumphant message of love of God and love of self and love of neighbor. Though, we are encouraged and even admonished to keep God's commandments, it is recognized that all have sinned and do sin and come short of God's glory. Where we have fallen short or when we do fall short, there is precious redemption in Christ's atoning sacrifice and in the scriptural doctrine of repentance which repentance in its simplest definition is change from doing what is wrong to doing what is right. This repentance is not suffering on our part because Jesus Christ has already suffered in Gethsemane and on the Cross for our sins. This repentance is not always restitution on our part because Jesus Christ alone as the Son of God was capable of restoring all things that are not just right. By the virtue and grace found in His atoning sacrifice in Gethsemane and on the Cross and by virtue of His glorious resurrection, He alone is able to bring us back to heaven to live with God. This repentance is and should include sorrow for our sins. And coupled with this great principle of repentance which brings us the joy of forgiveness is a plethora of scriptural passages that list and explain the many blessings and the great happiness God promises if and when we keep His commandments. Here are only three of those scriptures setting forth the great blessings and immense happiness we receive when we keep God's commandments:

"Isaiah Chapter 58 sets forth the blessings that come from observing a proper fast.
1 CRY aloud, spare not, lift up thy voice like a trumpet, and shew my people their transgression, and the house of Jacob their sins.

2 Yet they seek me daily, and delight to know my ways, as a nation that did righteousness, and forsook not the ordinance of their God: they ask of me the ordinances of justice; they take delight in approaching to God.

3 Wherefore have we fasted, say they, and thou seest not? wherefore have we afflicted our soul, and thou takest no knowledge? Behold, in the day of your fast ye find pleasure, and exact all your labours.

4 Behold, ye fast for strife and debate, and to smite with the fist of wickedness: ye shall not fast as ye do this day, to make your voice to be heard on high.

5 Is it such a fast that I have chosen? a day for a man to afflict his soul? is it to bow down his head as a bulrush, and to spread sackcloth and ashes under him? wilt thou call this a fast, and an acceptable day to the Lord?

6 Is not this the fast that I have chosen? to loose the bands of wickedness, to undo the heavy burdens, and to let the oppressed go free, and that ye break every yoke?

7 Is it not to deal thy bread to the hungry, and that thou bring the poor that are cast out to thy house? when thou seest the naked, that thou cover him; and that thou hide not thyself from thine own flesh?

8 **Then shall thy light break forth as the morning, and thine health shall spring forth speedily: and thy righteousness shall go before thee; the glory of the Lord shall be thy rereward.**

9 **Then shalt thou call, and the Lord shall answer; thou shalt cry, and he shall say, Here I am.** If thou take away from the midst of thee the yoke, the putting forth of the finger, and speaking vanity;

10 And if thou draw out thy soul to the hungry, and satisfy the afflicted soul; **then shall thy light rise in obscurity, and thy darkness be as the noonday:**

11 **And the Lord shall guide thee continually, and satisfy thy soul in drought, and make fat thy bones: and thou shalt be like a watered garden, and like a spring of water, whose waters fail not.**

12 **And they that shall be of thee shall build the old waste places: thou shalt raise up the foundations of many generations; and thou shalt be called, The repairer of the breach, The restorer of paths to dwell in.**

13 If thou turn away thy foot from the sabbath, from doing thy pleasure on my holy day; and call the sabbath a delight, the holy of the Lord, honourable; and shalt honour him, not doing thine own ways, nor finding thine own pleasure, nor speaking thine own words:

14 **Then shalt thou delight thyself in the Lord; and I will cause thee to ride upon the high places of the earth, and feed thee with the heritage of Jacob thy father: for the mouth of the Lord hath spoken it.**

"Isaiah Chapter 48 sets forth the blessings that come from keeping God's commandments.

18 O that thou hadst hearkened to my commandments! then had thy peace been as a river, and thy righteousness as the waves of the sea:

19 Thy seed also had been as the sand, and the offspring of thy bowels like the gravel thereof; his name should not have been cut off nor destroyed from before me.

"John Chapter 14 sets forth the magnificent blessings that come from loving God and keeping his commandments.

1 Let not your heart be troubled: ye believe in God, believe also in me.

2 In my Father's house are many mansions: if it were not so, I would have told you. I go to prepare a place for you.

3 And if I go and prepare a place for you, I will come again, and receive you unto myself; that where I am, there ye may be also.

...

13 And whatsoever ye shall ask in my name, that will I do, that the Father may be glorified in the Son.

14 If ye shall ask any thing in my name, I will do it.

15 If ye love me, keep my commandments.

16 And I will pray the Father, and he shall give you another Comforter, that he may abide with you for ever;

17 Even the Spirit of truth; whom the world cannot receive, because it seeth him not, neither knoweth him: but ye know him; for he dwelleth with you, and shall be in you.

18 I will not leave you comfortless: I will come to you.

...

27 Peace I leave with you, my peace I give unto you: not as the world giveth, give I unto you. Let not your heart be troubled, neither let it be afraid.

"My friends, there are consequences that derive from breaking or keeping God's commandments. His commandments are not just so many preferences to be observed and kept only if we feel like it. His commandments are given for our happiness. Breaking His commandments sooner than later brings loss of blessings including failure of prosperity and personal sorrow. Regular repentance and keeping God's commandments sooner than later bring us blessings not the least of which are positive family and neighbor relations, peace of mind , physical health and prosperity.

"In all of our conduct, "Would Jesus Christ Do That?" is the first question! "What Would Jesus Do?" is the second question!

Footnote (1) Bishop James favorite New Testament Gospel of John

THE GOSPEL OF JOHN   CHAPTER 1

Christ is the Word of God.

1 IN the beginning was the Word, and the Word was with God, and the Word was God.

2 The same was in the beginning with God.

3 All things were made by him; and without him was not any thing made that was made.

4 In him was life; and the life was the light of men.

5 And the light shineth in darkness; and the darkness comprehended it not.

6 There was a man sent from God, whose name was John.

7 The same came for a witness, to bear witness of the Light, that all men through him might believe.

8 He was not that Light, but was sent to bear witness of that Light.

9 That was the true Light, which lighteth every man that cometh into the world.

10 He was in the world, and the world was made by him, and the world knew him not.

11 He came unto his own, and his own received him not.

12 But as many as received him, to them gave he power to become the sons of God, even to them that believe on his name:

13 Which were born, not of blood, nor of the will of the flesh, nor of the will of man, but of God.

14 And the Word was made flesh, and dwelt among us, (and we beheld his glory, the glory as of the only begotten of the Father,) full of grace and truth.

15 John bare witness of him, and cried, saying, This was he of whom I spake, He that cometh after me is preferred before me: for he was before me.

16 And of his fulness have all we received, and grace for grace.

17 For the law was given by Moses, but grace and truth came by Jesus Christ.

18 No man hath seen God at any time; the only begotten Son, which is in the bosom of the Father, he hath declared him.

19 And this is the record of John, when the Jews sent priests and Levites from Jerusalem to ask him, Who art thou?

20 And he confessed, and denied not; but confessed, I am not the Christ.

21 And they asked him, What then? Art thou Elias? And he saith, I am not. Art thou that prophet? And he answered, No.

22 Then said they unto him, Who art thou? that we may give an answer to them that sent us. What sayest thou of thyself?

23 He said, I am the voice of one crying in the wilderness, Make straight the way of the Lord, as said the prophet Esaias.

24 And they which were sent were of the Pharisees.

25 And they asked him, and said unto him, Why baptizest thou then, if thou be not that Christ, nor Elias, neither that prophet?

26 John answered them, saying, I baptize with water: but there standeth one among you, whom ye know not;

27 He it is, who coming after me is preferred before me, whose shoe's latchet I am not worthy to unloose.

28 These things were done in Bethabara beyond Jordan, where John was baptizing.

29 The next day John seeth Jesus coming unto him, and saith, Behold the Lamb of God, which taketh away the sin of the world.

30 This is he of whom I said, After me cometh a man which is preferred before me: for he was before me.

31 And I knew him not: but that he should be made manifest to Israel, therefore am I come baptizing with water.

32 And John bare record, saying, I saw the Spirit descending from heaven like a dove, and it abode upon him.

33 And I knew him not: but he that sent me to baptize with water, the same said unto me, Upon whom thou shalt see the Spirit descending, and remaining on him, the same is he which baptizeth with the Holy Ghost.

34 And I saw, and bare record that this is the Son of God.

35 Again the next day after John stood, and two of his disciples;

36 And looking upon Jesus as he walked, he saith, Behold the Lamb of God!

37 And the two disciples heard him speak, and they followed Jesus.

38 Then Jesus turned, and saw them following, and saith unto them, **What seek ye?** They said unto him, Rabbi, (which is to say, being interpreted, Master,) where dwellest thou?

39 He saith unto them, **Come and see.** They came and saw where he dwelt, and abode with him that day: for it was about the tenth hour.

40 One of the two which heard John speak, and followed him, was Andrew, Simon Peter's brother.

41 He first findeth his own brother Simon, and saith unto him, We have found the Messias, which is, being interpreted, the Christ.

42 And he brought him to Jesus. And when Jesus beheld him, he said, **Thou art Simon the son of Jona: thou shalt be called Cephas,** which is by interpretation, A stone.

43 The day following Jesus would go forth into Galilee, and findeth Philip, and saith unto him, **Follow me.**

44 Now Philip was of Bethsaida, the city of Andrew and Peter.

45 Philip findeth Nathanael, and saith unto him, We have found him, of whom Moses in the law, and the prophets, did write, Jesus of Nazareth, the son of Joseph.

46 And Nathanael said unto him, Can there any good thing come out of Nazareth? Philip saith unto him, Come and see.

47 Jesus saw Nathanael coming to him, and saith of him, **Behold an Israelite indeed, in whom is no guile!**

48 Nathanael saith unto him, Whence knowest thou me? Jesus answered and said unto him, **Before that Philip called thee, when thou wast under the fig tree, I saw thee.**

49 Nathanael answered and saith unto him, Rabbi, thou art the Son of God; thou art the King of Israel.

50 Jesus answered and said unto him, **Because I said unto thee, I saw thee under the fig tree, believest thou? thou shalt see greater things than these.**

51 And he saith unto him, **Verily, verily, I say unto you, Hereafter ye shall see heaven open, and the angels of God ascending and descending upon the Son of man.**

THE GOSPEL OF JOHN   CHAPTER 2

Jesus turns water into wine in Cana.

1 AND the third day there was a marriage in Cana of Galilee; and the mother of Jesus was there:

2 And both Jesus was called, and his disciples, to the marriage.

3 And when they wanted wine, the mother of Jesus saith unto him, They have no wine.

4 Jesus saith unto her, **Woman, what have I to do with thee? mine hour is not yet come.**

5 His mother saith unto the servants, Whatsoever he saith unto you, do it.

6 And there were set there six waterpots of stone, after the manner of the purifying of the Jews, containing two or three firkins apiece.

7 Jesus saith unto them, **Fill the waterpots with water.** And they filled them up to the brim.

8 And he saith unto them, **Draw out now, and bear unto the governor of the feast**. And they bare it.

9 When the ruler of the feast had tasted the water that was made wine, and knew not whence it was: (but the servants which drew the water knew;) the governor of the feast called the bridegroom,

10 And saith unto him, Every man at the beginning doth set forth good wine; and when men have well drunk, then that which is worse: but thou hast kept the good wine until now.

11 This beginning of miracles did Jesus in Cana of Galilee, and manifested forth his glory; and his disciples believed on him.

12 After this he went down to Capernaum, he, and his mother, and his brethren, and his disciples: and they continued there not many days.

13 And the Jews' passover was at hand, and Jesus went up to Jerusalem,

14 And found in the temple those that sold oxen and sheep and doves, and the changers of money sitting:

15 And when he had made a scourge of small cords, he drove them all out of the temple, and the sheep, and the oxen; and poured out the changers' money, and overthrew the tables;

16 And said unto them that sold doves, **Take these things hence; make not my Father's house an house of merchandise.**

17 And his disciples remembered that it was written, The zeal of thine house hath eaten me up.

18 Then answered the Jews and said unto him, What sign shewest thou unto us, seeing that thou doest these things?

19 Jesus answered and said unto them, **Destroy this temple, and in three days I will raise it up.**

20 Then said the Jews, Forty and six years was this temple in building, and wilt thou rear it up in three days?

21 But he spake of the temple of his body.

22 When therefore he was risen from the dead, his disciples remembered that he had said this unto them; and they believed the scripture, and the word which Jesus had said.

23 Now when he was in Jerusalem at the passover, in the feast day, many believed in his name, when they saw the miracles which he did.

24 But Jesus did not commit himself unto them, because he knew all men,

25 And needed not that any should testify of man: for he knew what was in man.

THE GOSPEL OF JOHN   CHAPTER 3

Jesus tells Nicodemus men must be born again.

1 THERE was a man of the Pharisees, named Nicodemus, a ruler of the Jews:

2 The same came to Jesus by night, and said unto him, Rabbi, we know that thou art a teacher come from God: for no man can do these miracles that thou doest, except God be with him.

3 Jesus answered and said unto him, **Verily, verily, I say unto thee, Except a man be born again, he cannot see the kingdom of God.**

4 Nicodemus saith unto him, How can a man be born when he is old? can he enter the second time into his mother's womb, and be born?

5 Jesus answered, Verily, verily, **I say unto thee, Except a man be born of water and of the Spirit, he cannot enter into the kingdom of God.**

6 **That which is born of the flesh is flesh; and that which is born of the Spirit is spirit.**

7 **Marvel not that I said unto thee, Ye must be born again.**

8 **The wind bloweth where it listeth, and thou hearest the sound thereof, but canst not tell whence it cometh, and whither it goeth: so is every one that is born of the Spirit.**

9 Nicodemus answered and said unto him, How can these things be?

10 Jesus answered and said unto him, **Art thou a master of Israel, and knowest not these things?**

11 Verily, verily, I say unto thee, **We speak that we do know, and testify that we have seen; and ye receive not our witness.**

12 **If I have told you earthly things, and ye believe not, how shall ye believe, if I tell you of heavenly things?**

13 **And no man hath ascended up to heaven, but he that came down from heaven, even the Son of man which is in heaven.**

14 **And as Moses lifted up the serpent in the wilderness, even so must the Son of man be lifted up:**

15 **That whosoever believeth in him should not perish, but have eternal life.**

16 **For God so loved the world, that he gave his only begotten Son, that whosoever believeth in him should not perish, but have everlasting life.**

17 **For God sent not his Son into the world to condemn the world; but that the world through him might be saved.**

18 **He that believeth on him is not condemned: but he that believeth not is condemned already, because he hath not believed in the name of the only begotten Son of God.**

19 **And this is the condemnation, that light is come into the world, and men loved darkness rather than light, because their deeds were evil.**

20 **For every one that doeth evil hateth the light, neither cometh to the light, lest his deeds should be reproved.**

21 **But he that doeth truth cometh to the light, that his deeds may be made manifest, that they are wrought in God.**

22 After these things came Jesus and his disciples into the land of Judaea; and there he tarried with them, and baptized.

23 And John also was baptizing in Aenon near to Salim, because there was much water there: and they came, and were baptized.

24 For John was not yet cast into prison.

25 Then there arose a question between some of John's disciples and the Jews about purifying.

26 And they came unto John, and said unto him, Rabbi, he that was with thee beyond Jordan, to whom thou barest witness, behold, the same baptizeth, and all men come to him.

27 John answered and said, A man can receive nothing, except it be given him from heaven.

28 Ye yourselves bear me witness, that I said, I am not the Christ, but that I am sent before him.

29 He that hath the bride is the bridegroom: but the friend of the bridegroom, which standeth and heareth him, rejoiceth greatly because of the bridegroom's voice: this my joy therefore is fulfilled.

30 He must increase, but I must decrease.

31 He that cometh from above is above all: he that is of the earth is earthly, and speaketh of the earth: he that cometh from heaven is above all.

32 And what he hath seen and heard, that he testifieth; and no man receiveth his testimony.

33 He that hath received his testimony hath set to his seal that God is true.

34 For he whom God hath sent speaketh the words of God: for God giveth not the Spirit by measure unto him.

35 The Father loveth the Son, and hath given all things into his hand.

36 He that believeth on the Son hath everlasting life: and he that believeth not the Son shall not see life; but the wrath of God abideth on him.

THE GOSPEL OF JOHN   CHAPTER 4

Jesus teaches a woman of Samaria. Jesus heals a nobleman's son.

1 When therefore the Lord knew how the Pharisees had heard that Jesus made and baptized more disciples than John,

2 (Though Jesus himself baptized not, but his disciples,)

3 He left Judaea, and departed again into Galilee.

4 And he must needs go through Samaria.

5 Then cometh he to a city of Samaria, which is called Sychar, near to the parcel of ground that Jacob gave to his son Joseph.

6 Now Jacob's well was there. Jesus therefore, being wearied with his journey, sat thus on the well: and it was about the sixth hour.

7 There cometh a woman of Samaria to draw water: Jesus saith unto her, **Give me to drink.**

8 (For his disciples were gone away unto the city to buy meat.)

9 Then saith the woman of Samaria unto him, How is it that thou, being a Jew, askest drink of me, which am a woman of Samaria? for the Jews have no dealings with the Samaritans.

10 Jesus answered and said unto her, **If thou knewest the gift of God, and who it is that saith to thee, Give me to drink; thou wouldest have asked of him, and he would have given thee living water.**

11 The woman saith unto him, Sir, thou hast nothing to draw with, and the well is deep: from whence then hast thou that living water?

12 Art thou greater than our father Jacob, which gave us the well, and drank thereof himself, and his children, and his cattle?

13 Jesus answered and said unto her, **Whosoever drinketh of this water shall thirst again:**

14 **But whosoever drinketh of the water that I shall give him shall never thirst; but the water that I shall give him shall be in him a well of water springing up into everlasting life.**

15 The woman saith unto him, Sir, give me this water, that I thirst not, neither come hither to draw.

16 Jesus saith unto her, **Go, call thy husband, and come hither.**

17 The woman answered and said, I have no husband. Jesus said unto her, **Thou hast well said, I have no husband:**

18 **For thou hast had five husbands; and he whom thou now hast is not thy husband: in that saidst thou truly.**

19 The woman saith unto him, Sir, I perceive that thou art a prophet.

20 Our fathers worshipped in this mountain; and ye say, that in Jerusalem is the place where men ought to worship.

21 Jesus saith unto her, **Woman, believe me, the hour cometh, when ye shall neither in this mountain, nor yet at Jerusalem, worship the Father.**

22 **Ye worship ye know not what: we know what we worship: for salvation is of the Jews.**

23 **But the hour cometh, and now is, when the true worshippers shall worship the Father in spirit and in truth: for the Father seeketh such to worship him.**

24 **God is a Spirit: and they that worship him must worship him in spirit and in truth.**

25 The woman saith unto him, I know that Messias cometh, which is called Christ: when he is come, he will tell us all things.

26 Jesus saith unto her, **I that speak unto thee am he.**

27 And upon this came his disciples, and marvelled that he talked with the woman: yet no man said, What seekest thou? or, Why talkest thou with her?

28 The woman then left her waterpot, and went her way into the city, and saith to the men,

29 Come, see a man, which told me all things that ever I did: is not this the Christ?

30 Then they went out of the city, and came unto him.

31 In the mean while his disciples prayed him, saying, Master, eat.

32 But he said unto them, **I have meat to eat that ye know not of.**

33 Therefore said the disciples one to another, Hath any man brought him ought to eat?

34 Jesus saith unto them, **My meat is to do the will of him that sent me, and to finish his work.**

35 **Say not ye, There are yet four months, and then cometh harvest? behold, I say unto you, Lift up your eyes, and look on the fields; for they are white already to harvest.**

36 **And he that reapeth receiveth wages, and gathereth fruit unto life eternal: that both he that soweth and he that reapeth may rejoice together.**

37 **And herein is that saying true, One soweth, and another reapeth.**

38 **I sent you to reap that whereon ye bestowed no labour: other men laboured, and ye are entered into their labours.**

39 And many of the Samaritans of that city believed on him for the saying of the woman, which testified, He told me all that ever I did.

40 So when the Samaritans were come unto him, they besought him that he would tarry with them: and he abode there two days.

41 And many more believed because of his own word;

42 And said unto the woman, Now we believe, not because of thy saying: for we have heard him ourselves, and know that this is indeed the Christ, the Saviour of the world.

43 Now after two days he departed thence, and went into Galilee.

44 For Jesus himself testified, that a prophet hath no honour in his own country.

45 Then when he was come into Galilee, the Galilaeans received him, having seen all the things that he did at Jerusalem at the feast: for they also went unto the feast.

46 So Jesus came again into Cana of Galilee, where he made the water wine. And there was a certain nobleman, whose son was sick at Capernaum.

47 When he heard that Jesus was come out of Judaea into Galilee, he went unto him, and besought him that he would come down, and heal his son: for he was at the point of death.

48 Then said Jesus unto him, **Except ye see signs and wonders, ye will not believe.**

49 The nobleman saith unto him, Sir, come down ere my child die.

50 Jesus saith unto him, **Go thy way; thy son liveth.** And the man believed the word that Jesus had spoken unto him, and he went his way.

51 And as he was now going down, his servants met him, and told him, saying, Thy son liveth.

52 Then enquired he of them the hour when he began to amend. And they said unto him, Yesterday at the seventh hour the fever left him.

53 So the father knew that it was at the same hour, in the which Jesus said unto him, Thy son liveth: and himself believed, and his whole house.

54 This is again the second miracle that Jesus did, when he was come out of Judaea into Galilee.

THE GOSPEL OF JOHN   CHAPTER 5

Jesus heals an invalid on the Sabbath.

1 AFTER this there was a feast of the Jews; and Jesus went up to Jerusalem.

2 Now there is at Jerusalem by the sheep market a pool, which is called in the Hebrew tongue Bethesda, having five porches.

3 In these lay a great multitude of impotent folk, of blind, halt, withered, waiting for the moving of the water.

4 For an angel went down at a certain season into the pool, and troubled the water: whosoever then first after the troubling of the water stepped in was made whole of whatsoever disease he had.

5 And a certain man was there, which had an infirmity thirty and eight years.

6 When Jesus saw him lie, and knew that he had been now a long time in that case, he saith unto him, **Wilt thou be made whole?**

7 The impotent man answered him, Sir, I have no man, when the water is troubled, to put me into the pool: but while I am coming, another steppeth down before me.

8 Jesus saith unto him, **Rise, take up thy bed, and walk.**

9 And immediately the man was made whole, and took up his bed, and walked: and on the same day was the sabbath.

10 The Jews therefore said unto him that was cured, It is the sabbath day: it is not lawful for thee to carry thy bed.

11 He answered them, He that made me whole, the same said unto me, Take up thy bed, and walk.

12 Then asked they him, What man is that which said unto thee, Take up thy bed, and walk?

13 And he that was healed wist not who it was: for Jesus had conveyed himself away, a multitude being in that place.

14 Afterward Jesus findeth him in the temple, and said unto him, **Behold, thou art made whole: sin no more, lest a worse thing come unto thee.**

15 The man departed, and told the Jews that it was Jesus, which had made him whole.

16 And therefore did the Jews persecute Jesus, and sought to slay him, because he had done these things on the sabbath day.

17 But Jesus answered them, **My Father worketh hitherto, and I work.**

18 Therefore the Jews sought the more to kill him, because he not only had broken the sabbath, but said also that God was his Father, making himself equal with God.

19 Then answered Jesus and said unto them, **Verily, verily, I say unto you, The Son can do nothing of himself, but what he seeth the Father do: for what things soever he doeth, these also doeth the Son likewise.**

20 **For the Father loveth the Son, and sheweth him all things that himself doeth: and he will shew him greater works than these, that ye may marvel.**

21 **For as the Father raiseth up the dead, and quickeneth them; even so the Son quickeneth whom he will.**

22 **For the Father judgeth no man, but hath committed all judgment unto the Son:**

23 **That all men should honour the Son, even as they honour the Father. He that honoureth not the Son honoureth not the Father which hath sent him.**

24 **Verily, verily, I say unto you, He that heareth my word, and believeth on him that sent me, hath everlasting life, and shall not come into condemnation; but is passed from death unto life.**

25 **Verily, verily, I say unto you, The hour is coming, and now is, when the dead shall hear the voice of the Son of God: and they that hear shall live.**

26 **For as the Father hath life in himself; so hath he given to the Son to have life in himself;**

27 **And hath given him authority to execute judgment also, because he is the Son of man.**

28 Marvel not at this: for the hour is coming, in the which all that are in the graves shall hear his voice,

29 And shall come forth; they that have done good, unto the resurrection of life; and they that have done evil, unto the resurrection of damnation.

30 I can of mine own self do nothing: as I hear, I judge: and my judgment is just; because I seek not mine own will, but the will of the Father which hath sent me.

31 If I bear witness of myself, my witness is not true.

32 There is another that beareth witness of me; and I know that the witness which he witnesseth of me is true.

33 Ye sent unto John, and he bare witness unto the truth.

34 But I receive not testimony from man: but these things I say, that ye might be saved.

35 He was a burning and a shining light: and ye were willing for a season to rejoice in his light.

36 But I have greater witness than that of John: for the works which the Father hath given me to finish, the same works that I do, bear witness of me, that the Father hath sent me.

37 And the Father himself, which hath sent me, hath borne witness of me. Ye have neither heard his voice at any time, nor seen his shape.

38 And ye have not his word abiding in you: for whom he hath sent, him ye believe not.

39 Search the scriptures; for in them ye think ye have eternal life: and they are they which testify of me.

40 And ye will not come to me, that ye might have life.

41 I receive not honour from men.

42 But I know you, that ye have not the love of God in you.

43 I am come in my Father's name, and ye receive me not: if another shall come in his own name, him ye will receive.

44 How can ye believe, which receive honour one of another, and seek not the honour that cometh from God only?

45 Do not think that I will accuse you to the Father: there is one that accuseth you, even Moses, in whom ye trust.

46 For had ye believed Moses, ye would have believed me: for he wrote of me.

47 But if ye believe not his writings, how shall ye believe my words?

THE GOSPEL OF JOHN   CHAPTER 6

Jesus feeds the five thousand.

1 AFTER these things Jesus went over the sea of Galilee, which is the sea of Tiberias.

2 And a great multitude followed him, because they saw his miracles which he did on them that were diseased.

3 And Jesus went up into a mountain, and there he sat with his disciples.

4 And the passover, a feast of the Jews, was nigh.

5 When Jesus then lifted up his eyes, and saw a great company come unto him, he saith unto Philip, **Whence shall we buy bread, that these may eat?**

6 And this he said to prove him: for he himself knew what he would do.

7 Philip answered him, Two hundred pennyworth of bread is not sufficient for them, that every one of them may take a little.

8 One of his disciples, Andrew, Simon Peter's brother, saith unto him,

9 There is a lad here, which hath five barley loaves, and two small fishes: but what are they among so many?

10 And Jesus said, **Make the men sit down.** Now there was much grass in the place. So the men sat down, in number about five thousand.

11 And Jesus took the loaves; and when he had given thanks, he distributed to the disciples, and the disciples to them that were set down; and likewise of the fishes as much as they would.

12 When they were filled, he said unto his disciples, **Gather up the fragments that remain, that nothing be lost.**

13 Therefore they gathered them together, and filled twelve baskets with the fragments of the five barley loaves, which remained over and above unto them that had eaten.

14 Then those men, when they had seen the miracle that Jesus did, said, This is of a truth that prophet that should come into the world.

15 When Jesus therefore perceived that they would come and take him by force, to make him a king, he departed again into a mountain himself alone.

16 And when even was now come, his disciples went down unto the sea,

17 And entered into a ship, and went over the sea toward Capernaum. And it was now dark, and Jesus was not come to them.

18 And the sea arose by reason of a great wind that blew.

19 So when they had rowed about five and twenty or thirty furlongs, they see Jesus walking on the sea, and drawing nigh unto the ship: and they were afraid.

20 But he saith unto them, **It is I; be not afraid.**

21 Then they willingly received him into the ship: and immediately the ship was at the land whither they went.

22 The day following, when the people which stood on the other side of the sea saw that there was none other boat there, save that one whereinto his disciples were entered, and that Jesus went not with his disciples into the boat, but that his disciples were gone away alone;

23 (Howbeit there came other boats from Tiberias nigh unto the place where they did eat bread, after that the Lord had given thanks:)

24 When the people therefore saw that Jesus was not there, neither his disciples, they also took shipping, and came to Capernaum, seeking for Jesus.

25 And when they had found him on the other side of the sea, they said unto him, Rabbi, when camest thou hither?

26 Jesus answered them and said, **Verily, verily, I say unto you, Ye seek me, not because ye saw the miracles, but because ye did eat of the loaves, and were filled.**

27 **Labour not for the meat which perisheth, but for that meat which endureth unto everlasting life, which the Son of man shall give unto you: for him hath God the Father sealed.**

28 Then said they unto him, What shall we do, that we might work the works of God?

29 Jesus answered and said unto them, **This is the work of God, that ye believe on him whom he hath sent.**

30 They said therefore unto him, What sign shewest thou then, that we may see, and believe thee? what dost thou work?

31 Our fathers did eat manna in the desert; as it is written, He gave them bread from heaven to eat.

32 Then Jesus said unto them, **Verily, verily, I say unto you, Moses gave you not that bread from heaven; but my Father giveth you the true bread from heaven.**

33 **For the bread of God is he which cometh down from heaven, and giveth life unto the world.**

34 Then said they unto him, Lord, evermore give us this bread.

35 And Jesus said unto them, **I am the bread of life: he that cometh to me shall never hunger; and he that believeth on me shall never thirst.**

36 **But I said unto you, That ye also have seen me, and believe not.**

37 **All that the Father giveth me shall come to me; and him that cometh to me I will in no wise cast out.**

38 **For I came down from heaven, not to do mine own will, but the will of him that sent me.**

39 **And this is the Father's will which hath sent me, that of all which he hath given me I should lose nothing, but should raise it up again at the last day.**

40 **And this is the will of him that sent me, that every one which seeth the Son, and believeth on him, may have everlasting life: and I will raise him up at the last day.**

41 The Jews then murmured at him, because he said, I am the bread which came down from heaven.

42 And they said, Is not this Jesus, the son of Joseph, whose father and mother we know? how is it then that he saith, I came down from heaven?

43 Jesus therefore answered and said unto them, **Murmum not among yourselves.**

44 **No man can come to me, except the Father which hath sent me draw him: and I will raise him up at the last day.**

45 **It is written in the prophets, And they shall be all taught of God. Every man therefore that hath heard, and hath learned of the Father, cometh unto me.**

46 **Not that any man hath seen the Father, save he which is of God, he hath seen the Father.**

47 **Verily, verily, I say unto you, He that believeth on me hath everlasting life.**

48 **I am that bread of life.**

49 **Your fathers did eat manna in the wilderness, and are dead.**

50 **This is the bread which cometh down from heaven, that a man may eat thereof, and not die.**

51 **I am the living bread which came down from heaven: if any man eat of this bread, he shall live for ever: and the bread that I will give is my flesh, which I will give for the life of the world.**

52 The Jews therefore strove among themselves, saying, How can this man give us his flesh to eat?

53 Then Jesus said unto them, **Verily, verily, I say unto you, Except ye eat the flesh of the Son of man, and drink his blood, ye have no life in you.**

54 **Whoso eateth my flesh, and drinketh my blood, hath eternal life; and I will raise him up at the last day.**

55 **For my flesh is meat indeed, and my blood is drink indeed.**

56 **He that eateth my flesh, and drinketh my blood, dwelleth in me, and I in him.**

57 **As the living Father hath sent me, and I live by the Father: so he that eateth me, even he shall live by me.**

58 **This is that bread which came down from heaven: not as your fathers did eat manna, and are dead: he that eateth of this bread shall live for ever.**

59 These things said he in the synagogue, as he taught in Capernaum.

60 Many therefore of his disciples, when they had heard this, said, This is an hard saying; who can hear it?

61 When Jesus knew in himself that his disciples murmured at it, he said unto them, **Doth this offend you?**

62 **What and if ye shall see the Son of man ascend up where he was before?**

63 **It is the spirit that quickeneth; the flesh profiteth nothing: the words that I speak unto you, they are spirit, and they are life.**

64 **But there are some of you that believe not.** For Jesus knew from the beginning who they were that believed not, and who should betray him.

65 And he said, **Therefore said I unto you, that no man can come unto me, except it were given unto him of my Father.**

66 From that time many of his disciples went back, and walked no more with him.

67 Then said Jesus unto the twelve, **Will ye also go away?**

68 Then Simon Peter answered him, Lord, to whom shall we go? thou hast the words off eternal life.

69 And we believe and are sure that thou art that Christ, the Son of the living God.

70 Jesus answered them, **Have not I chosen you twelve, and one of you is a devil?**

71 He spake of Judas Iscariot the son of Simon: for he it was that should betray him, being one of the twelve.

THE GOSPEL OF JOHN   CHAPTER 7

Jesus' kinsmen believe not.

1 AFTER these things Jesus walked in Galilee: for he would not walk in Jewry, because the Jews sought to kill him.

2 Now the Jews' feast of tabernacles was at hand.

3 His brethren therefore said unto him, Depart hence, and go into Judaea, that thy disciples also may see the works that thou doest.

4 For there is no man that doeth any thing in secret, and he himself seeketh to be known openly. If thou do these things, shew thyself to the world.

5 For neither did his brethren believe in him.

6 Then Jesus said unto them, **My time is not yet come: but your time is alway ready.**

7 **The world cannot hate you; but me it hateth, because I testify of it, that the works thereof are evil.**

8 **Go ye up unto this feast: I go not up yet unto this feast; for my time is not yet full come.**

9 When he had said these words unto them, he abode still in Galilee.

10 But when his brethren were gone up, then went he also up unto the feast, not openly, but as it were in secret.

11 Then the Jews sought him at the feast, and said, Where is he?

12 And there was much murmuring among the people concerning him: for some said, He is a good man: others said, Nay; but he deceiveth the people.

13 Howbeit no man spake openly of him for fear of the Jews.

14 Now about the midst of the feast Jesus went up into the temple, and taught.

15 And the Jews marvelled, saying, How knoweth this man letters, having never learned?

16 Jesus answered them, and said, **My doctrine is not mine, but his that sent me.**

17 **If any man will do his will, he shall know of the doctrine, whether it be of God, or whether I speak of myself.**

18 **He that speaketh of himself seeketh his own glory: but he that seeketh his glory that sent him, the same is true, and no unrighteousness is in him.**

19 **Did not Moses give you the law, and yet none of you keepeth the law? Why go ye about to kill me?**

20 The people answered and said, Thou hast a devil: who goeth about to kill thee?

21 Jesus answered and said unto them, **I have done one work, and ye all marvel.**

22 **Moses therefore gave unto you circumcision; (not because it is of Moses, but of the fathers;) and ye on the sabbath day circumcise a man.**

23 **If a man on the sabbath day receive circumcision, that the law of Moses should not be broken; are ye angry at me, because I have made a man every whit whole on the sabbath day?**

24 **Judge not according to the appearance, but judge righteous judgment.**

25 Then said some of them of Jerusalem, Is not this he, whom they seek to kill?

26 But, lo, he speaketh boldly, and they say nothing unto him. Do the rulers know indeed that this is the very Christ?

27 Howbeit we know this man whence he is: but when Christ cometh, no man knoweth whence he is.

28 Then cried Jesus in the temple as he taught, saying, **Ye both know me, and ye know whence I am: and I am not come of myself, but he that sent me is true<u>true</u>, whom ye know not.**

29 **But I know him: for I am from him, and he hath sent me.**

30 Then they sought to take him: but no man laid hands on him, because his hour was not yet come.

31 And many of the people believed on him, and said, When Christ cometh, will he do more miracles than these which this man hath done?

32 The Pharisees heard that the people murmured such things concerning him; and the Pharisees and the chief priests sent officers to take him.

33 Then said Jesus unto them, **Yet a little while am I with you, and then I go unto him that sent me.**

34 Ye shall seek me, and shall not find me: and where I am, thither ye cannot come.

35 Then said the Jews among themselves, Whither will he go, that we shall not find him? will he go unto the dispersed among the Gentiles, and teach the Gentiles?

36 What manner of saying is this that he said, Ye shall seek me, and shall not find me: and where I am, thither ye cannot come?

37 In the last day, that great day of the feast, Jesus stood and cried, saying, **If any man thirst, let him come unto me, and drink.**

38 **He that believeth on me, as the scripture hath said, out of his belly shall flow rivers of living water.**

39 (But this spake he of the Spirit, which they that believe on him should receive: for the Holy Ghost was not yet given; because that Jesus was not yet glorified.)

40 Many of the people therefore, when they heard this saying, said, Of a truth this is the Prophet.

41 Others said, This is the Christ. But some said, Shall Christ come out of Galilee?

42 Hath not the scripture said, That Christ cometh of the seed of David, and out of the town of Bethlehem, where David was?

43 So there was a division among the people because of him.

44 And some of them would have taken him; but no man laid hands on him.

45 Then came the officers to the chief priests and Pharisees; and they said unto them, Why have ye not brought him?

46 The officers answered, Never man spake like this man.

47 Then answered them the Pharisees, Are ye also deceived?

48 Have any of the rulers or of the Pharisees believed on him?

49 But this people who knoweth not the law are cursed.

50 Nicodemus saith unto them, (he that came to Jesus by night, being one of them,)

51 Doth our law judge any man, before it hear him, and know what he doeth?

52 They answered and said unto him, Art thou also of Galilee? Search, and look: for out of Galilee ariseth no prophet.

53 And every man went unto his own house.

THE GOSPEL OF JOHN CHAPTER 8

The woman taken in adultery. 'Before Abraham was I Jehovah.'

1 JESUS went unto the mount of Olives.

2 And early in the morning he came again into the temple, and all the people came unto him; and he sat down, and taught them.

3 And the scribes and Pharisees brought unto him a woman taken in adultery; and when they had set her in the midst,

4 They say unto him, Master, this woman was taken in adultery, in the very act.

5 Now Moses in the law commanded us, that such should be stoned: but what sayest thou?

6 This they said, tempting him, that they might have to accuse him. But Jesus stooped down, and with his finger wrote on the ground, as though he heard them not.

7 So when they continued asking him, he lifted up himself, and said unto them, **He that is without sin among you, let him first cast a stone at her.**

8 And again he stooped down, and wrote on the ground.

9 And they which heard it, being convicted by their own conscience, went out one by one, beginning at the eldest, even unto the last: and Jesus was left alone, and the woman standing in the midst.

10 When Jesus had lifted up himself, and saw none but the woman, he said unto her, **Woman, where are those thine accusers? hath no man condemned thee?**

11 She said, No man, Lord. And Jesus said unto her, **Neither do I condemn thee: go, and sin no more.**

12 Then spake Jesus again unto them, saying, **I am the light of the world: he that followeth me shall not walk in darkness, but shall have the light of life.**

13 The Pharisees therefore said unto him, Thou bearest record of thyself; thy record is not true.

14 Jesus answered and said unto them, **Though I bear record of myself, yet my record is true: for I know whence I came, and whither I go; but ye cannot tell whence I come, and whither I go.**

15 **Ye judge after the flesh; I judge no man.**

16 **And yet if I judge, my judgment is true: for I am not alone, but I and the Father that sent me.**

17 **It is also written in your law, that the testimony of two men is true.**

18 **I am one that bear witness of myself, and the Father that sent me beareth witness of me.**

19 Then said they unto him, Where is thy Father? Jesus answered, **Ye neither know me, nor my Father: if ye had known me, ye should have known my Father also.**

20 These words spake Jesus in the treasury, as he taught in the temple: and no man laid hands on him; for his hour was not yet come.

21 Then said Jesus again unto them, **I go my way, and ye shall seek me, and shall die in your sins: whither I go, ye cannot come.**

22 Then said the Jews, Will he kill himself? because he saith, Whither I go, ye cannot come.

23 And he said unto them, **Ye are from beneath; I am from above: ye are of this world; I am not of this world.**

24 **I said therefore unto you, that ye shall die in your sins: for if ye believe not that I am he, ye shall die in your sins.**

25 Then said they unto him, Who art thou? And Jesus saith unto them, **Even the same that I said unto you from the beginning.**

26 **I have many things to say and to judge of you: but he that sent me is true; and I speak to the world those things which I have heard of him.**

27 They understood not that he spake to them of the Father.

28 Then said Jesus unto them, **When ye have lifted up the Son of man, then shall ye know that I am he, and that I do nothing of myself; but as my Father hath taught me, I speak these things.**

29 **And he that sent me is with me: the Father hath not left me alone; for I ^cdo always those things that please him.**

30 As he spake these words, many believed on him.

31 Then said Jesus to those Jews which believed on him, **If ye continue in my word, then are ye my disciples indeed;**

32 **And ye shall know the truth, and the truth shall make you free.**

33 They answered him, We be Abraham's's seed, and were never in bondage to any man: how sayest thou, Ye shall be made free?

34 Jesus answered them, **Verily, verily, I say unto you, Whosoever committeth sin is the servant of sin.**

35 **And the servant abideth not in the house for ever: but the Son abideth ever.**

36 **If the Son therefore shall make you free, ye shall be free indeed.**

37 **I know that ye are Abraham's seed; but ye seek to kill me, because my word hath no place in you.**

38 **I speak that which I have seen with my Father: and ye do that which ye have seen with your father.**

39 They answered and said unto him, Abraham is our father. Jesus saith unto them, **If ye were Abraham's children, ye would do the works of Abraham.**

40 **But now ye seek to kill me, a man that hath told you the truth, which I have heard of God: this did not Abraham.**

41 **Ye do the deeds of your father.** Then said they to him, We be not born of fornication; we have one Father, even God.

42 Jesus said unto them, **If God were your Father, ye would love me: for I proceeded forth and came from God; neither came I of myself, but he sent me.**

43 **Why do ye not understand my speech? even because ye cannot hear my word.**

44 **Ye are of your father the devil, and the lusts of your father ye will do. He was a murderer from the beginning, and abode not in the truth, because there is no truth in him. When he speaketh a lie, he speaketh of his own: for he is a lier, and the father of it.**

45 **And because I tell you the truth, ye believe me not.**

46 **Which of you convinceth me of sin? And if I say the truth, why do ye not believe me?**

47 **He that is of God heareth God's words: ye therefore hear them not, because ye are not of God.**

48 Then answered the Jews, and said unto him, Say we not well that thou art a Samaritan, and hast a devil?

49 Jesus answered, **I have not a devil; but I honour my Father, and ye do dishonour me.**

50 **And I seek not mine own glory: there is one that seeketh and judgeth.**

51 **Verily, verily, I say unto you, If a man keep my saying, he shall never see death.**

52 Then said the Jews unto him, Now we know that thou hast a devil. Abraham is dead, and the prophets; and thou sayest, If a man keep my saying, he shall never taste of death.

53 Art thou greater than our father Abraham, which is dead? and the prophets are dead: whom makest thou thyself?

54 Jesus answered, **If I honour myself, my honour is nothing: it is my Father that honoureth me; of whom ye say, that he is your God:**

55 **Yet ye have not known him; but I know him: and if I should say, I know him not, I shall be a liar like unto you: but I know him, and keep his saying.**

56 **Your father Abraham rejoiced to see my day: and he saw it, and was glad.**

57 Then said the Jews unto him, Thou art not yet fifty years old, and hast thou seen Abraham?

58 Jesus said unto them, **Verily, verily, I say unto you, Before Abraham was, I am.**

59 Then took they up stones to cast at him: but Jesus hid himself, and went out of the temple, going through the midst of them, and so passed by.

THE GOSPEL OF JOHN CHAPTER 9

Jesus, on the Sabbath, heals a man born blind.

1 AND as Jesus passed by, he saw a man which was blind from his birth.

2 And his disciples asked him, saying, Master, who did sin, this man, or his parents, that he was born blind?

3 Jesus answered, **Neither hath this man sinned, nor his parents: but that the works of God should be made manifest in him.**

4 **I must work the works of him that sent me, while it is day: the night cometh, when no man can work.**

5 **As long as I am in the world, I am the light of the world.**

6 When he had thus spoken, he spat on the ground, and made clay of the spittle, and he anointed the eyes of the blind man with the clay,

7 And said unto him, **Go, wash in the pool of Siloam,** (which is by interpretation, Sent.) He went his way therefore, and washed, and came seeing.

8 The neighbours therefore, and they which before had seen him that he was blind, said, Is not this he that sat and begged?

9 Some said, This is he: others said, He is like him: but he said, I am he.

10 Therefore said they unto him, How were thine eyes opened?

11 He answered and said, A man that is called Jesus made clay, and anointed mine eyes, and said unto me, Go to the pool of Siloam, and wash: and I went and washed, and I received sight.

12 Then said they unto him, Where is he? He said, I know not.

13 They brought to the Pharisees him that aforetime was blind.

14 And it was the sabbath day when Jesus made the clay, and opened his eyes.

15 Then again the Pharisees also asked him how he had received his sight. He said unto them, He put clay upon mine eyes, and I washed, and do see.

16 Therefore said some of the Pharisees, This man is not of God, because he keepeth not the sabbath day. Others said, How can a man that is a sinner do such miracles? And there was a division among them.

17 They say unto the blind man again, What sayest thou of him, that he hath opened thine eyes? He said, He is a prophet.

18 But the Jews did not believe concerning him, that he had been blind, and received his sight, until they called the parents of him that had received his sight.

19 And they asked them, saying, Is this your son, who ye say was born blind? how then doth he now see?

20 His parents answered them and said, We know that this is our son, and that he was born blind:

21 But by what means he now seeth, we know not; or who hath opened his eyes, we know not: he is of age; ask him: he shall speak for himself.

22 These words spake his parents, because they feared the Jews: for the Jews had agreed already, that if any man did confess that he was Christ, he should be put out of the synagogue.

23 Therefore said his parents, He is of age; ask him.

24 Then again called they the man that was blind, and said unto him, Give God the praise: we know that this man is a sinner.

25 He answered and said, Whether he be a sinner or no, I know not: one thing I know, that, whereas I was blind, now I see.

26 Then said they to him again, What did he to thee? how opened he thine eyes?

27 He answered them, I have told you already, and ye did not hear: wherefore would ye hear it again? will ye also be his disciples?

28 Then they reviled him, and said, Thou art his disciple; but we are Moses' disciples.

29 We know that God spake unto Moses: as for this fellow, we know not from whence he is.

30 The man answered and said unto them, Why herein is a marvellous thing, that ye know not from whence he is, and yet he hath opened mine eyes.

31 Now we know that God heareth not sinners: but if any man be a worshipper of God, and doeth his will, him he heareth.

32 Since the world began was it not heard that any man opened the eyes of one that was born blind.

33 If this man were not of God, he could do nothing.

34 They answered and said unto him, Thou wast altogether born in sins, and dost thou teach us? And they cast him out.

35 Jesus heard that they had cast him out; and when he had found him, he said unto him, **Dost thou believe on the Son of God?**

36 He answered and said, Who is he, Lord, that I might believe on him?

37 And Jesus said unto him, **Thou hast both seen him, and it is he that talketh with thee.**

38 And he said, Lord, I believe. And he worshipped him.

39 And Jesus said, **For judgment I am come into this world, that they which see not might see; and that they which see might be made blind.**

40 And some of the Pharisees which were with him heard these words, and said unto him, Are we blind also?

41 Jesus said unto them, **If ye were blind, ye should have no sin: but now ye say, We see; therefore your sin remaineth.**

THE GOSPEL OF JOHN   CHAPTER 10

Jesus is the good Shepherd. He proclaims: 'I am the Son of God.'

1 VERILY, **verily, I say unto you, He that entereth not by the door into the sheepfold, but climbeth up some other way, the same is a thief and a robber.**

2 **But he that entereth in by the door is the shepherd of the sheep.**

3 To him the porter openeth; and the sheep hear his voice: and he calleth his own sheep by name, and leadeth them out.

4 **And when he putteth forth his own sheep, he goeth before them, and the sheep follow him: for they know his voice.**

5 **And a stranger will they not follow, but will flee from him: for they know not the voice of strangers.**

6 This parable spake Jesus unto them: but they understood not what things they were which he spake unto them.

7 Then said Jesus unto them again, **Verily, verily, I say unto you, I am the door of the sheep.**

8 **All that ever came before me are thieves and robbers: but the sheep did not hear them.**

9 **I am the door: by me if any man enter in, he shall be saved, and shall go in and out, and find pasture.**

10 **The thief cometh not, but for to steal, and to kill, and to destroy: I am come that they might have life, and that they might have it more abundantly.**

11 **I am the good shepherd: the good shepherd giveth his life for the sheep.**

12 **But he that is an hireling, and not the shepherd, whose own the sheep are not, seeth the wolf coming, and leaveth the sheep, and fleeth: and the wolf catcheth them, and scattereth the sheep.**

13 **The hireling fleeth, because he is an hireling, and careth not for the sheep.**

14 **I am the good shepherd, and know my sheep, and am known of mine.**

15 **As the Father knoweth me, even so know I the Father: and I lay down my life for the sheep.**

16 **And other sheep I have, which are not of this fold: them also I must bring, and they shall hear my voice; and there shall be one fold, and one shepherd.**

17 **Therefore doth my Father love me, because I lay down my life, that I might take it again.**

18 **No man taketh it from me, but I lay it down of myself. I have power to lay it down, and I have power to take it again. This commandment have I received of my Father.**

19 There was a division therefore again among the Jews for these sayings.

20 And many of them said, He hath a devil, and is mad; why hear ye him?

21 Others said, These are not the words of him that hath a devil. Can a devil open the eyes of the blind?

22 And it was at Jerusalem the feast of the dedication, and it was winter.

23 And Jesus walked in the temple in Solomon's porch.

24 Then came the Jews round about him, and said unto him, How long dost thou make us to doubt? If thou be the Christ, tell us plainly.

25 Jesus answered them, **I told you, and ye believed not: the works that I do in my Father's name, they bear witness of me.**

26 **But ye believe not, because ye are not of my sheep, as I said unto you.**

27 **My sheep hear my voice, and I know them, and they follow me:**

28 **And I give unto them eternal life; and they shall never perish, neither shall any man pluck them out of my hand.**

29 **My Father, which gave them me, is greater than all; and no man is able to pluck them out of my Father's hand.**

30 **I and my Father are one.**

31 Then the Jews took up stones again to stone him.

32 Jesus answered them, **Many good works have I shewed you from my Father; for which of those works do ye stone me?**

33 The Jews answered him, saying, For a good work we stone thee not; but for blasphemy; and because that thou, being a man, makest thyself God.

34 Jesus answered them, **Is it not written in your law, I said, Ye are gods?**

35 **If he called them gods, unto whom the word of God came, and the scripture cannot be broken;**

36 **Say ye of him, whom the Father hath sanctified, and sent into the world, Thou blasphemest; because I said, I am the Son of God?**

37 **If I do not the works of my Father, believe me not.**

38 **But if I do, though ye believe not me, believe the works: that ye may know, and believe, that the Father is in me, and I in him.**

39 Therefore they sought again to take him: but he escaped out of their hand,

40 And went away again beyond Jordan into the place where John at first baptized; and there he abode.

41 And many resorted unto him, and said, John did no miracle: but all things that John spake of this man were true.

42 And many believed on him there.

THE GOSPEL OF JOHN   CHAPTER 11

Jesus testifies he is the resurrection and the life. He raises Lazarus from the dead. Caiaphas speaks prophetically of the death of Christ.

1 Now a certain man was sick, named Lazarus, of Bethany, the town of Mary and her sister Martha.

2 (It was that Mary which anointed the Lord with ointment, and wiped his feet with her hair, whose brother Lazarus was sick.)

3 Therefore his sisters sent unto him, saying, Lord, behold, he whom thou lovest is sick.

4 When Jesus heard that, he said, **This sickness is not unto death, but for the glory of God, that the Son of God might be glorified thereby.**

5 Now Jesus loved Martha, and her sister, and Lazarus.

6 When he had heard therefore that he was sick, he abode two days still in the same place where he was.

7 Then after that saith he to his disciples, **Let us go into Judaea again.**

8 His disciples say unto him, Master, the Jews of late sought to stone thee; and goest thou thither again?

9 Jesus answered, **Are there not twelve hours in the day? If any man walk in the day, he stumbleth not, because he seeth the light of this world.**

10 **But if a man walk in the night, he stumbleth, because there is no light in him.**

11 These things said he: and after that he saith unto them, **Our friend Lazarus sleepeth; but I go, that I may awake him out of sleep.**

12 Then said his disciples, Lord, if he sleep, he shall do well.

13 Howbeit Jesus spake of his death: but they thought that he had spoken of taking of rest in sleep.

14 Then said Jesus unto them plainly, **Lazarus is dead.**

15 **And I am glad for your sakes that I was not there, to the intent ye may believe; nevertheless let us go unto him.**

16 Then said Thomas, which is called Didymus, unto his fellowdisciples, Let us also go, that we may die with him.

17 Then when Jesus came, he found that he had lain in the grave four days already.

18 Now Bethany was nigh unto Jerusalem, about fifteen furlongs off:

19 And many of the Jews came to Martha and Mary, to comfort them concerning their brother.

20 Then Martha, as soon as she heard that Jesus was coming, went and met him: but Mary sat still in the house.

21 Then said Martha unto Jesus, Lord, if thou hadst been here, my brother had not died.

22 But I know, that even now, whatsoever thou wilt ask of God, God will give it thee.

23 Jesus saith unto her, **Thy brother shall rise again.**

24 Martha saith unto him, I know that he shall rise again in the resurrection at the last day.

25 Jesus said unto her, **I am the resurrection, and the life: he that believeth in me, though he were dead, yet shall he live:**

26 **And whosoever liveth and believeth in me shall never die. Believest thou this?**

27 **She saith unto him, Yea, Lord: I believe that thou art the Christ, the Son of God, which should come into the world.**

28 And when she had so said, she went her way, and called Mary her sister secretly, saying, The Master is come, and calleth for thee.

29 As soon as she heard that, she arose quickly, and came unto him.

30 Now Jesus was not yet come into the town, but was in that place where Martha met him.

31 The Jews then which were with her in the house, and comforted her, when they saw Mary, that she rose up hastily and went out, followed her, saying, She goeth unto the grave to weep there.

32 Then when Mary was come where Jesus was, and saw him, she fell down at his feet, saying unto him, Lord, if thou hadst been here, my brother had not died.

33 When Jesus therefore saw her weeping, and the Jews also weeping which came with her, he groaned in the spirit, and was troubled,

34 And said, **Where have ye laid him?** They said unto him, Lord, come and see.

35 Jesus wept.

36 Then said the Jews, Behold how he loved him!

37 And some of them said, Could not this man, which opened the eyes of the blind, have caused that even this man should not have died?

38 Jesus therefore again groaning in himself cometh to the grave. It was a cave, and a stone lay upon it.

39 Jesus said, **Take ye away the stone.** Martha, the sister of him that was dead, saith unto him, Lord, by this time he stinketh: for he hath been dead four days.

40 Jesus saith unto her, **Said I not unto thee, that, if thou wouldest believe, thou shouldest see the glory of God?**

41 Then they took away the stone from the place where the dead was laid. And Jesus lifted up his eyes, and said, **Father, I thank thee that thou hast heard me.**

42 **And I knew that thou hearest me always: but because of the people which stand by I said it, that they may believe that thou hast sent me.**

43 And when he thus had spoken, he cried with a loud voice, **Lazarus, come forth.**

44 And he that was dead came forth, bound hand and foot with graveclothes: and his face was bound about with a napkin. Jesus saith unto them, **Loose him, and let him go.**

45 Then many of the Jews which came to Mary, and had seen the things which Jesus did, believed on him.

46 But some of them went their ways to the Pharisees, and told them what things Jesus had done.

47 Then gathered the chief priests and the Pharisees a council, and said, What do we? for this man doeth many miracles.

48 If we let him thus alone, all men will believe on him: and the Romans shall come and take away both our place and nation.

49 And one of them, named Caiaphas, being the high priest that same year, said unto them, Ye know nothing at all,

50 Nor consider that it is expedient for us, that one man should die for the people, and that the whole nation perish not.

51 And this spake he not of himself: but being high priest that year, he prophesied that Jesus should die for that nation;

52 And not for that nation only, but that also he should gather together in one the children of God that were scattered abroad.

53 Then from that day forth they took counsel together for to put him to death.

54 Jesus therefore walked no more openly among the Jews; but went thence unto a country near to the wilderness, into a city called Ephraim, and there continued with his disciples.

55 And the Jews' passover was nigh at hand: and many went out of the country up to Jerusalem before the passover, to purify themselves.

56 Then sought they for Jesus, and spake among themselves, as they stood in the temple, What think ye, that he will not come to the feast?

57 Now both the chief priests and the Pharisees had given a commandment, that, if any man knew where he were, he should shew it, that they might take him.

THE GOSPEL OF JOHN CHAPTER 12

Mary anoints Jesus' feet. He foretells his death.

1 THEN Jesus six days before the passover came to Bethany, where Lazarus was which had been dead, whom he raised from the dead.

2 There they made him a supper; and Martha served: but Lazarus was one of them that sat at the table with him.

3 Then took Mary a pound of ointment of spikenard, very costly, and anointed the feet of Jesus, and wiped his feet with her hair: and the house was filled with the odour of the ointment.

4 Then saith one of his disciples, Judas Iscariot, Simon's son, which should betray him,

5 Why was not this ointment sold for three hundred pence, and given to the poor?

6 This he said, not that he cared for the poor; but because he was a thief, and had the bag, and bare what was put therein.

7 Then said Jesus, **Let her alone: against the day of my burying hath she kept this.**

8 For the poor always ye have with you; but me ye have not always.

9 Much people of the Jews therefore knew that he was there: and they came not for Jesus' sake only, but that they might see Lazarus also, whom he had raised from the dead.

10 But the chief priests consulted that they might put Lazarus also to death;

11 Because that by reason of him many of the Jews went away, and believed on Jesus.

12 On the next day much people that were come to the feast, when they heard that Jesus was coming to Jerusalem,

13 Took branches of palm trees, and went forth to meet him, and cried, Hosanna: Blessed is the King of Israel that cometh in the name of the Lord.

14 And Jesus, when he had found a young ass, sat thereon; as it is written,

15 Fear not, daughter of Sion: behold, thy King cometh, sitting on an ass's colt.

16 These things understood not his disciples at the first: but when Jesus was glorified, then remembered they that these things were written of him, and that they had done these things unto him.

17 The people therefore that was with him when he called Lazarus out of his grave, and raised him from the dead, bare record.

18 For this cause the people also met him, for that they heard that he had done this miracle.

19 The Pharisees therefore said among themselves, Perceive ye how ye prevail nothing? behold, the world is gone after him.

20 And there were certain Greeks among them that came up to worship at the feast:

21 The same came therefore to Philip, which was of Bethsaida of Galilee, and desired him, saying, Sir, we would see Jesus.

22 Philip cometh and telleth Andrew: and again Andrew and Philip tell Jesus.

23 And Jesus answered them, saying, **The hour is come, that the Son of man should be glorified.**

24 **Verily, verily, I say unto you, Except a corn of wheat fall into the ground and die, it abideth alone: but if it die, it bringeth forth much fruit.**

25 **He that loveth his life shall lose it; and he that hateth his life in this world shall keep it unto life eternal.**

26 **If any man serve me, let him follow me; and where I am, there shall also my servant be: if any man serve me, him will my Father honour.**

27 **Now is my soul troubled; and what shall I say? Father, save me from this hour: but for this cause came I unto this hour.**

28 **Father, glorify thy name. Then came there a voice from heaven, saying, I have both glorified it, and will glorify it again.**

29 The people therefore, that stood by, and heard it, said that it thundered: others said, An angel spake to him.

30 Jesus answered and said, **This voice came not because of me, but for your sakes.**

31 **Now is the judgment of this world: now shall the prince of this world be cast out.**

32 **And I, if I be lifted up from the earth, will draw all men unto me.**

33 This he said, signifying what death he should die.

34 The people answered him, We have heard out of the law that Christ abideth for ever: and how sayest thou, The Son of man must be lifted up? who is this Son of man?

35 Then Jesus said unto them, **Yet a little while is the light with you. Walk while ye have the light, lest darkness come upon you: for he that walketh in darkness knoweth not whither he goeth.**

36 **While ye have light, believe in the light, that ye may be the children of light.** These things spake Jesus, and departed, and did hide himself from them.

37 But though he had done so many miracles before them, yet they believed not on him:

38 That the saying of Esaias the prophet might be fulfilled, which he spake, Lord, who hath believed our report? and to whom hath the arm of the Lord been revealed?

39 Therefore they could not believe, because that Esaias said again,

40 He hath blinded their eyes, and hardened their heart; that they should not see with their eyes, nor understand with their heart, and be converted, and I should heal them.

41 These things said Esaias, when he saw his glory, and spake of him.

42 Nevertheless among the chief rulers also many believed on him; but because of the Pharisees they did not confess him, lest they should be put out of the synagogue:

43 For they loved the praise of men more than the praise of God.

44 Jesus cried and said, **He that believeth on me, believeth not on me, but on him that sent me.**

45 **And he that seeth me seeth him that sent me.**

46 **I am come a light into the world, that whosoever believeth on me should not abide in darkness.**

47 **And if any man hear my words, and believe not, I judge him not: for I came not to judge the world, but to save the world.**

48 **He that rejecteth me, and receiveth not my words, hath one that judgeth him: the word that I have spoken, the same shall judge him in the last day.**

49 **For I have not spoken of myself; but the Father which sent me, he gave me a commandment, what I should say, and what I should speak.**

50 **And I know that his commandment is life everlasting: whatsoever I speak therefore, even as the Father said unto me, so I speak.**

Jesus washes the feet of the Twelve. He identifies Judas as his betrayer. He commands them to love one another.

1 Now before the feast of the passover, when Jesus knew that his hour was come that he should depart out of this world unto the Father, having loved his own which were in the world, he loved them unto the end.

2 And supper being ended, the devil having now put into the heart of Judas Iscariot, Simon's son, to betray him;

3 Jesus knowing that the Father had given all things into his hands, and that he was come from God, and went to God;

4 He riseth from supper, and laid aside his garments; and took a towel, and girded himself.

5 After that he poureth water into a bason, and began to wash the disciples' feet, and to wipe them with the towel wherewith he was girded.

6 Then cometh he to Simon Peter: and Peter saith unto him, Lord, dost thou wash my feet?

7 Jesus answered and said unto him, **What I do thou knowest not now; but thou shalt know hereafter.**

8 Peter saith unto him, Thou shalt never wash my feet. Jesus answered him, **If I wash thee not, thou hast no part with me.**

9 Simon Peter saith unto him, Lord, not my feet only, but also my hands and my head.

10 Jesus saith to him, **He that is washed needeth not save to wash his feet, but is clean every whit: and ye are clean, but not all.**

11 For he knew who should betray him; therefore said he, Ye are not all clean.

12 So after he had washed their feet, and had taken his garments, and was set down again, he said unto them, **Know ye what I have done to you?**

13 **Ye call me Master and Lord: and ye say well; for so I am.**

14 **If I then, your Lord and Master, have washed your feet; ye also ought to wash one another's feet.**

15 **For I have given you an example, that ye should do as I have done to you.**

16 **Verily, verily, I say unto you, The servant is not greater than his lord; neither he that is sent greater than he that sent him.**

17 **If ye know these things, happy are ye if ye do them.**

18 **I speak not of you all: I know whom I have chosen: but that the scripture may be fulfilled, He that eateth bread with me hath lifted up his heel against me.**

19 **Now I tell you before it come, that, when it is come to pass, ye may believe that I am he.**

20 **Verily, verily, I say unto you, He that receiveth whomsoever I send receiveth me; and he that receiveth me receiveth him that sent me.**

21 When Jesus had thus said, he was troubled in spirit, and testified, and said, **Verily, verily, I say unto you, that one of you shall betray me.**

22 Then the disciples looked one on another, doubting of whom he spake.

23 Now there was leaning on Jesus' bosom one of his disciples, whom Jesus loved.

24 Simon Peter therefore beckoned to him, that he should ask who it should be of whom he spake.

25 He then lying on Jesus' breast saith unto him, Lord, who is it?

26 Jesus answered, **He it is, to whom I shall give a sop, when I have dipped it.** And when he had dipped the sop, he gave it to Judas Iscariot, the son of Simon.

27 And after the sop Satan entered into him. Then said Jesus unto him, **That thou doest, do quickly.**

28 Now no man at the table knew for what intent he spake this unto him.

29 For some of them thought, because Judas had the bag, that Jesus had said unto him, Buy those things that we have need of against the feast; or, that he should give something to the poor.

30 He then having received the sop went immediately out: and it was night.

31 Therefore, when he was gone out, Jesus said, **Now is the Son of man glorified, and God is glorified in him.**

32 **If God be glorified in him, God shall also glorify him in himself, and shall straightway glorify him.**

33 **Little children, yet a little while I am with you. Ye shall seek me: and as I said unto the Jews, Whither I go, ye cannot come; so now I say to you.**

34 **A new commandment I give unto you, That ye love one another; as I have loved you, that ye also love one another.**

35 **By this shall all men know that ye are my disciples, if ye have love one to another.**

36 Simon Peter said unto him, Lord, whither goest thou? Jesus answered him, **Whither I go, thou canst not follow me now; but thou shalt follow me afterwards.**

37 Peter said unto him, Lord, why cannot I follow thee now? I will lay down my life for thy sake.

38 Jesus answered him, **Wilt thou lay down thy life for my sake? Verily, verily, I say unto thee, The cock shall not crow, till thou hast denied me thrice.**

THE GOSPEL OF JOHN   CHAPTER 14

Jesus speaks of many mansions. He is the way, the truth, and the life. He promises the first and second Comforters.

1 LET not your heart be troubled: ye believe in God, believe also in me.

2 **In my Father's house are many mansions: if it were not so, I would have told you. I go to prepare a place for you.**

3 **And if I go and prepare a place for you, I will come again, and receive you unto myself; that where I am, there ye may be also.**

4 **And whither I go ye know, and the way ye know.**

5 Thomas saith unto him, Lord, we know not whither thou goest; and how can we know the way?

6 Jesus saith unto him, **I am the way, the truth, and the life: no man cometh unto the Father, but by me.**

7 **If ye had known me, ye should have known my Father also: and from henceforth ye know him, and have seen him.**

8 Philip saith unto him, Lord, shew us the Father, and it sufficeth us.

9 Jesus saith unto him, **Have I been so long time with you, and yet hast thou not known me, Philip? he that hath seen me hath seen the Father; and how sayest thou then, Shew us the Father?**

10 **Believest thou not that I am in the Father, and the Father in me? the words that I speak unto you I speak not of myself: but the Father that dwelleth in me, he doeth the works.**

11 **Believe me that I am in the Father, and the Father in me: or else believe me for the very works' sake.**

12 **Verily, verily, I say unto you, He that believeth on me, the works that I do shall he do also; and greater works than these shall he do; because I go unto my Father.**

13 **And whatsoever ye shall ask in my name, that will I do, that the Father may be glorified in the Son.**

14 **If ye shall ask any thing in my name, I will do it.**

15 **If ye love me, keep my commandments.**

16 **And I will pray the Father, and he shall give you another Comforter, that he may abide with you for ever;**

17 **Even the Spirit of truth; whom the world cannot receive, because it seeth him not, neither knoweth him: but ye know him; for he dwelleth with you, and shall be in you.**

18 **I will not leave you comfortless: I will come to you.**

19 **Yet a little while, and the world seeth me no more; but ye see me: because I live, ye shall live also.**

20 **At that day ye shall know that I am in my Father, and ye in me, and I in you.**

21 **He that hath my commandments, and keepeth them, he it is that loveth me: and he that loveth me shall be loved of my Father, and I will love him, and will manifest myself to him.**

22 Judas saith unto him, not Iscariot, Lord, how is it that thou wilt manifesting thyself unto us, and not unto the world?

23 Jesus answered and said unto him, **If a man love me, he will keep my words: and my Father will love him, and we will come unto him, and make our abode with him.**

24 **He that loveth me not keepeth not my sayings: and the word which ye hear is not mine, but the Father's which sent me.**

25 **These things have I spoken unto you, being yet present with you.**

26 **But the Comforter, which is the Holy Ghost, whom the Father will send in my name, he shall teach you all things, and bring all things to your remembrance, whatsoever I have said unto you.**

27 **Peace I leave with you, my peace I give unto you: not as the world giveth, give I unto you. Let not your heart be troubled, neither let it be afraid.**

28 **Ye have heard how I said unto you, I go away, and come again unto you. If ye loved me, ye would rejoice, because I said, I go unto the Father: for my Father is greater than I.**

29 **And now I have told you before it come to pass, that, when it is come to pass, ye might believe.**

30 **Hereafter I will not talk much with you: for the prince of this world cometh, and hath nothing in me.**

31 **But that the world may know that I love the Father; and as the Father gave me commandment, even so I do. Arise, let us go hence.**

Jesus is the vine. We his disciples are the branches. He discourses on perfect law of love. His servants have been chosen and ordained by him. The world hates and fights true religion. The promise of the Comforter, the Spirit of truth.

1 I AM the true vine, and my Father is the husbandman.

2 Every branch in me that beareth not fruit he taketh away: and every branch that beareth fruit, he purgeth it, that it may bring forth more fruit.

3 Now ye are clean through the word which I have spoken unto you.

4 Abide in me, and I in you. As the branch cannot bear fruit of itself, except it abide in the vine; no more can ye, except ye abide in me.

5 I am the vine, ye are the branches: He that abideth in me, and I in him, the same bringeth forth much fruit: for without me ye can do nothing.

6 If a man abide not in me, he is cast forth as a branch, and is withered; and men gather them, and cast them into the fire, and they are burned.

7 If ye abide in me, and my words abide in you, ye shall ask what ye will, and it shall be done unto you.

8 Herein is my Father glorified, that ye bear much fruit; so shall ye be my disciples.

9 As the Father hath loved me, so have I loved you: continue ye in my love.

10 If ye keep my commandments, ye shall abide in my love; even as I have kept my Father's commandments, and abide in his love.

11 These things have I spoken unto you, that my joy might remain in you, and that your [a]joy might be full.

12 This is my commandment, That ye love one another, as I have loved you.

13 Greater love hath no man than this, that a man lay down his life for his friends.

14 Ye are my friends, if ye do whatsoever I command you.

15 Henceforth I call you not servants; for the servant knoweth not what his lord doeth: but I have called you friends; for all things that I have heard of my Father I have made known unto you.

16 Ye have not chosen me, but I have chosen you, and ordained you, that ye should go and bring forth fruit, and that your fruit should remain: that whatsoever ye shall ask of the Father in my name, he may give it you.

17 These things I command you, that ye love one another.

18 If the world hate you, ye know that it hated me before it hated you.

19 If ye were of the world, the world would love his own: but because ye are not of the world, but I have chosen you out of the world, therefore the world hateth you.

20 Remember the word that I said unto you, The servant is not greater than his lord. If they have persecuted me, they will also persecute you; if they have kept my saying, they will keep yours also.

21 But all these things will they do unto you for my name's sake, because they know not him that sent me.

22 If I had not come and spoken unto them, they had not had sin: but now they have no cloke for their sin.

23 He that hateth me hateth my Father also.

24 If I had not done among them the works which none other man did, they had not had sin: but now have they both seen and hated both me and my Father.

25 But this cometh to pass, that the word might be fulfilled that is written in their law, They hated me without a cause.

26 But when the Comforter is come, whom I will send unto you from the Father, even the Spirit of truth, which proceedeth from the Father, he shall testify of me:

27 And ye also shall bear witness, because ye have been with me from the beginning.

THE GOSPEL OF JOHN   CHAPTER 16

Jesus discourses on mission of Holy Ghost. He tells of his death and resurrection. He announces his own divine Sonship. He says he has overcome the world.

1 THESE things have I spoken unto you, that ye should not be offended.

2 They shall put you out of the synagogues: yea, the time cometh, that whosoever killeth you will think that he doeth God service.

3 And these things will they do unto you, because they have not known the Father, nor me.

4 But these things have I told you, that when the time shall come, ye may remember that I told you of them. And these things I said not unto you at the beginning, because I was with you.

5 But now I go my way to him that sent me; and none of you asketh me, Whither goest thou?

6 But because I have said these things unto you, sorrow hath filled your heart.

7 Nevertheless I tell you the truth; It is expedient for you that I go away: for if I go not away, the Comforter will not come unto you; but if I depart, I will send him unto you.

8 And when he is come, he will reprove the world of sin, and of righteousness, and of judgment:

9 Of sin, because they believe not on me;

10 Of righteousness, because I go to my Father, and ye see me no more;

11 Of judgment, because the prince of this world is judged.

12 I have yet many things to say unto you, but ye cannot bear them now.

13 Howbeit when he, the Spirit of truth, is come, he will guide you into all truth: for he shall not speak of himself; but whatsoever he shall hear, that shall he speak: and he will shew you things to come.

14 He shall glorify me: for he shall receive of mine, and shall shew it unto you.

15 All things that the Father hath are mine: therefore said I, that he shall take of mine, and shall shew it unto you.

16 A little while, and ye shall not see me: and again, a little while, and ye shall see me, because I go to the Father.

17 Then said some of his disciples among themselves, What is this that he saith unto us, A little while, and ye shall not see me: and again, a little while, and ye shall see me: and, Because I go to the Father?

18 They said therefore, What is this that he saith, A little while? we cannot tell what he saith.

19 Now Jesus knew that they were desirous to ask him, and said unto them, **Do ye enquire among yourselves of that I said, A little while, and ye shall not see me: and again, a little while, and ye shall see me?**

20 **Verily, verily, I say unto you, That ye shall weep and lament, but the world shall rejoice: and ye shall be sorrowful, but your sorrow shall be turned into joy.**

21 **A woman when she is in travail hath sorrow, because her hour is come: but as soon as she is delivered of the child, she remembereth no more the anguish, for joy that a man is born into the world.**

22 **And ye now therefore have sorrow: but I will see you again, and your heart shall rejoice, and your joy no man taketh from you.**

23 **And in that day ye shall ask me nothing. Verily, verily, I say unto you, Whatsoever ye shall ask the Father in my name, he will give it you.**

24 **Hitherto have ye asked nothing in my name: ask, and ye shall receive, that your joy may be full.**

25 **These things have I spoken unto you in proverbs: but the time cometh, when I shall no more speak unto you in proverbs, but I shall shew you plainly of the Father.**

26 **At that day ye shall ask in my name: and I say not unto you, that I will pray the Father for you:**

27 **For the Father himself loveth you, because ye have loved me, and have believed that I came out from God.**

28 **I came forth from the Father, and am come into the world: again, I leave the world, and go to the Father.**

29 His disciples said unto him, Lo, now speakest thou plainly, and speakest no proverb.

30 Now are we sure that thou knowest all things, and needest not that any man should ask thee: by this we believe that thou camest forth from God.

31 Jesus answered them, **Do ye now believe?**

32 **Behold, the hour cometh, yea, is now come, that ye shall be scattered, every man to his own, and shall leave me alone: and yet I am not alone, because the Father is with me.**

33 **These things I have spoken unto you, that in me ye might have peace. In the world ye shall have tribulation: but be of good cheer; I have overcome the world.**

THE GOSPEL OF JOHN   CHAPTER 17

Jesus offers the great intercessory prayer. He is glorified by gaining eternal life. He prays for his apostles and all the saints. How the Father and Son are one.

1 THESE words spake Jesus, and lifted up his eyes to heaven, and said, **Father, the hour is come; glorify thy Son, that thy Son also may glorify thee:**

2 **As thou hast given him power over all flesh, that he should give eternal life to as many as thou hast given him.**

3 **And this is life eternal, that they might know thee the only true God, and Jesus Christ, whom thou hast sent.**

4 I have glorified thee on the earth: I have finished the work which thou gavest me to do.

5 And now, O Father, glorify thou me with thine own self with the glory which I had with thee before the world was.

6 I have manifested thy name unto the men which thou gavest me out of the world: thine they were, and thou gavest them me; and they have kept thy word.

7 Now they have known that all things whatsoever thou hast given me are of thee.

8 For I have given unto them the words which thou gavest me; and they have received them, and have known surely that I came out from thee, and they have believed that thou didst send me.

9 I pray for them: I pray not for the world, but for them which thou hast given me; for they are thine.

10 And all mine are thine, and thine are mine; and I am glorified in them.

11 And now I am no more in the world, but these are in the world, and I come to thee. Holy Father, keep through thine own name those whom thou hast given me, that they may be one, as we are.

12 While I was with them in the world, I kept them in thy name: those that thou gavest me I have kept, and none of them is lost, but the son of perdition; that the scripture might be fulfilled.

13 And now come I to thee; and these things I speak in the world, that they might have my joy fulfilled in themselves.

14 I have given them thy word; and the world hath hated them, because they are not of the world, even as I am not of the world.

15 I pray not that thou shouldest take them out of the world, but that thou shouldest [b]<u>keep</u> them from the evil.

16 They are not of the world, even as I am not of the world.

17 Sanctify them through thy truth: thy word is truth.

18 As thou hast sent me into the world, even so have I also sent them into the world.

19 And for their sakes I sanctify myself, that they also might be sanctified through the truth.

20 Neither pray I for these alone, but for them also which shall believe on me through their word;

21 That they all may be one; as thou, Father, art in me, and I in thee, that they also may be one in us: that the world may believe that thou hast sent me.

22 And the glory which thou gavest me I have given them; that they may be one, even as we are one:

23 I in them, and thou in me, that they may be made perfect in one; and that the world may know that thou hast sent me, and hast loved them, as thou hast loved me.

24 Father, I will that they also, whom thou hast given me, be with me where I am; that they may behold my glory, which thou hast given me: for thou lovedst me before the foundation of the world.

25 O righteous Father, the world hath not known thee: but I have known thee, and these have known that thou hast sent me.

26 And I have declared unto them thy name, and will declare it: that the love wherewith thou hast loved me may be in them, and I in them.

THE GOSPEL OF JOHN   CHAPTER 18

Jesus is betrayed and arrested. He is examined and maltreated first before Annas, then before Caiaphas. Peter denies knowing who Jesus is. Jesus is arraigned before Pilate.

1 WHEN Jesus had spoken these words, he went forth with his disciples over the brook Cedron, where was a garden, into the which he entered, and his disciples.

2 And Judas also, which betrayed him, knew the place: for Jesus ofttimes resorted thither with his disciples.

3 Judas then, having received a band of men and officers from the chief priests and Pharisees, cometh thither with lanterns and torches and weapons.

4 Jesus therefore, knowing all things that should come upon him, went forth, and said unto them, **Whom seek ye?**

5 They answered him, Jesus of Nazareth. Jesus saith unto them, **I am he.** And Judas also, which betrayed him, stood with them.

6 As soon then as he had said unto them, **I am he,** they went backward, and fell to the ground.

7 Then asked he them again, **Whom seek ye?** And they said, Jesus of Nazareth.

8 Jesus answered, **I have told you that I am he: if therefore ye seek me, let these go their way:**

9 That the saying might be fulfilled, which he spake, **Of them which thou gavest me have I lost none.**

10 Then Simon Peter having a sword drew it, and smote the high priest's servant, and cut off his right ear. The servant's name was Malchus.

11 Then said Jesus unto Peter, **Put up thy sword into the sheath: the cup which my Father hath given me, shall I not drink it?**

12 Then the band and the captain and officers of the Jews took Jesus, and bound him,

13 And led him away to Annas first; for he was father in law to Caiaphas, which was the high priest that same year.

14 Now Caiaphas was he, which gave counsel to the Jews, that it was expedient that one man should die for the people.

15 And Simon Peter followed Jesus, and so did another disciple: that disciple was known unto the high priest, and went in with Jesus into the palace of the high priest.

16 But Peter stood at the door without. Then went out that other disciple, which was known unto the high priest, and spake unto her that kept the door, and brought in Peter.

17 Then saith the damsel that kept the door unto Peter, Art not thou also one of this man's disciples? He saith, I am not.

18 And the servants and officers stood there, who had made a fire of coals; for it was cold: and they warmed themselves: and Peter stood with them, and warmed himself.

19 The high priest then asked Jesus of his disciples, and of his doctrine.

20 Jesus answered him, **I spake openly to the world; I ever taught in the synagogue, and in the temple, whither the Jews always resort; and in secret have I said nothing.**

21 **Why askest thou me? ask them which heard me, what I have said unto them: behold, they know what I said.**

22 And when he had thus spoken, one of the officers which stood by struck Jesus with the palm of his hand, saying, Answerest thou the high priest so?

23 Jesus answered him, **If I have spoken evil, bear witness of the evil: but if well, why smitest thou me?**

24 Now Annas had sent him bound unto Caiaphas the high priest.

25 And Simon Peter stood and warmed himself. They said therefore unto him, Art not thou also one of his disciples? He denied it, and said, I am not.

26 One of the servants of the high priest, being his kinsman whose ear Peter cut off, saith, Did not I see thee in the garden with him?

27 Peter then denied again: and immediately the cock crew.

28 Then led they Jesus from Caiaphas unto the hall of judgment: and it was early; and they themselves went not into the judgment hall, lest they should be defiled; but that they might eat the passover.

29 Pilate then went out unto them, and said, What accusation bring ye against this man?

30 They answered and said unto him, If he were not a malefactor, we would not have delivered him up unto thee.

31 Then said Pilate unto them, Take ye him, and judge him according to your law. The Jews therefore said unto him, It is not lawful for us to put any man to death:

32 That the saying of Jesus might be fulfilled, which he spake, signifying what death he should die.

33 Then Pilate entered into the judgment hall again, and called Jesus, and said unto him, Art thou the King of the Jews?

34 Jesus answered him, **Sayest thou this thing of thyself, or did others tell it thee of me?**

35 Pilate answered, Am I a Jew? Thine own nation and the chief priests have delivered thee unto me: what hast thou done?

36 Jesus answered, **My kingdom is not of this world: if my kingdom were of this world, then would my servants fight, that I should not be delivered to the Jews: but now is my kingdom not from hence.**

37 Pilate therefore said unto him, Art thou a king then? Jesus answered, **Thou sayest that I am a king. To this end was I born, and for this cause came I into the world, that I should bear witness unto the truth. Every one that is of the truth heareth my voice.**

38 Pilate saith unto him, What is truth? And when he had said this, he went out again unto the Jews, and saith unto them, I find in him no fault at all.

39 But ye have a custom, that I should release unto you one at the passover: will ye therefore that I release unto you the King of the Jews?

40 Then cried they all again, saying, Not this man, but Barabbas. Now Barabbas was a robber.

Jesus is scourged and crucified. He places his mother in John's care. He dies. He is buried in the tomb of Joseph of Arimathaea.

1 THEN Pilate therefore took Jesus, and scourged him.

2 And the soldiers platted a crown of thorns, and put it on his head, and they put on him a purple robe,

3 And said, Hail, King of the Jews! and they smote him with their hands.

4 Pilate therefore went forth again, and saith unto them, Behold, I bring him forth to you, that ye may know that I find no fault in him.

5 Then came Jesus forth, wearing the crown of thorns, and the purple robe. And Pilate saith unto them, Behold the man!

6 When the chief priests therefore and officers saw him, they cried out, saying, Crucify him, crucify him. Pilate saith unto them, Take ye him, and crucify him: for I find no fault in him.

7 The Jews answered him, We have a law, and by our law he ought to die, because he made himself the Son of God.

8 When Pilate therefore heard that saying, he was the more afraid;

9 And went again into the judgment hall, and saith unto Jesus, Whence art thou? But Jesus gave him no answer.

10 Then saith Pilate unto him, Speakest thou not unto me? knowest thou not that I have power to crucify thee, and have power to release thee?

11 Jesus answered, **Thou couldest have no power at all against me, except it were given thee from above: therefore he that delivered me unto thee hath the greater sin.**

12 And from thenceforth Pilate sought to release him: but the Jews cried out, saying, If thou let this man go, thou art not Caesar's friend: whosoever maketh himself a king speaketh against Caesar.

13 When Pilate therefore heard that saying, he brought Jesus forth, and sat down in the judgment seat in a place that is called the Pavement, but in the Hebrew, Gabbatha.

14 And it was the preparation of the passover, and about the sixth hour: and he saith unto the Jews, Behold your King!

15 But they cried out, Away with him, away with him, crucify him. Pilate saith unto them, Shall I crucify your King? The chief priests answered, We have no king but Caesar.

16 Then delivered he him therefore unto them to be crucified. And they took Jesus, and led him away.

17 And he bearing his cross went forth into a place called the place of a skull, which is called in the Hebrew Golgotha:

18 Where they crucified him, and two other with him, on either side one, and Jesus in the midst.

19 And Pilate wrote a title, and put it on the cross. And the writing was, JESUS OF NAZARETH THE KING OF THE JEWS.

20 This title then read many of the Jews: for the place where Jesus was crucified was nigh to the city: and it was written in Hebrew, and Greek, and Latin.

21 Then said the chief priests of the Jews to Pilate, Write not, The King of the Jews; but that he said, I am King of the Jews.

22 Pilate answered, What I have written I have written.

23 Then the soldiers, when they had crucified Jesus, took his garments, and made four parts, to every soldier a part; and also his coat: now the coat was without seam, woven from the top throughout.

24 They said therefore among themselves, Let us not rend it, but cast lots for it, whose it shall be: that the scripture might be fulfilled, which saith, They parted my raiment among them, and for my vesture they did cast lots. These things therefore the soldiers did.

25 Now there stood by the cross of Jesus his mother, and his mother's sister, Mary the wife of Cleopas, and Mary Magdalene.

26 When Jesus therefore saw his mother, and the disciple standing by, whom he loved, he saith unto his mother, **Woman, behold thy son!**

27 Then saith he to the disciple, **Behold thy mother!** And from that hour that disciple took her unto his own home.

28 After this, Jesus knowing that all things were now accomplished, that the scripture might be fulfilled, saith, **I thirst**.

29 Now there was set a vessel full of vinegar: and they filled a spunge with vinegar, and put it upon hyssop, and put it to his mouth.

30 When Jesus therefore had received the vinegar, he said, **It is finished**: and he bowed his head, and gave up the ghost.

31 The Jews therefore, because it was the preparation, that the bodies should not remain upon the cross on the sabbath day, (for that sabbath day was an high day,) besought Pilate that their legs might be broken, and that they might be taken away.

32 Then came the soldiers, and brake the legs of the first, and of the other which was crucified with him.

33 But when they came to Jesus, and saw that he was dead already, they brake not his legs:

34 But one of the soldiers with a spear pierced his side, and forthwith came there out blood and water.

35 And he that saw it bare record, and his record is true: and he knoweth that he saith true, that ye might believe.

36 For these things were done, that the scripture should be fulfilled, A bone of him shall not be broken.

37 And again another scripture saith, They shall look on him whom they pierced.

38 And after this Joseph of Arimathaea, being a disciple of Jesus, but secretly for fear of the Jews, besought Pilate that he might take away the body of Jesus: and Pilate gave him leave. He came therefore, and took the body of Jesus.

39 And there came also Nicodemus, which at the first came to Jesus by night, and brought a mixture of myrrh and aloes, about an hundred pound weight.

40 Then took they the body of Jesus, and wound it in linen clothes with the spices, as the manner of the Jews is to bury.

41 Now in the place where he was crucified there was a garden; and in the garden a new sepulchre, wherein was never man yet laid.

42 There laid they Jesus therefore because of the Jews' preparation day; for the sepulchre was nigh at hand.

Mary Magdalene, Peter, John find empty tomb. The Risen Christ appears to Mary Magdalene in the garden. He appears to disciples and shows his resurrected body. Thomas feels the wounds in Jesus' hands, feet, and side. 'Jesus is the Christ, the Son of God.'

1 THE first day of the week cometh Mary Magdalene early, when it was yet dark, unto the sepulchre, and seeth the stone taken away from the sepulchre.

2 Then she runneth, and cometh to Simon Peter, and to the other disciple, whom Jesus loved, and saith unto them, They have taken away the Lord out of the sepulchre, and we know not where they have laid him.

3 Peter therefore went forth, and that other disciple, and came to the sepulchre.

4 So they ran both together: and the other disciple did outrun Peter, and came first to the sepulchre.

5 And he stooping down, and looking in, saw the linen clothes lying; yet went he not in.

6 Then cometh Simon Peter following him, and went into the sepulchre, and seeth the linen clothes lie,

7 And the napkin, that was about his head, not lying with the linen clothes, but wrapped together in a place by itself.

8 Then went in also that other disciple, which came first to the sepulchre, and he saw, and believed.

9 For as yet they knew not the scripture, that he must rise again from the dead.

10 Then the disciples went away again unto their own home.

11 But Mary stood without at the sepulchre weeping: and as she wept, she stooped down, and looked into the sepulchre,

12 And seeth two angels in white sitting, the one at the head, and the other at the feet, where the body of Jesus had lain.

13 And they say unto her, Woman, why weepest thou? She saith unto them, Because they have taken away my Lord, and I know not where they have laid him.

14 And when she had thus said, she turned herself back, and saw Jesus standing, and knew not that it was Jesus.

15 Jesus saith unto her, **Woman, why weepest thou? whom seekest thou?** She, supposing him to be the gardener, saith unto him, Sir, if thou have borne him hence, tell me where thou hast laid him, and I will take him away.

16 Jesus saith unto her, **Mary**. She turned herself, and saith unto him, Rabboni; which is to say, Master.

17 Jesus saith unto her, **Touch me not; for I am not yet ascended to my Father: but go to my brethren, and say unto them, I ascend unto my Father, and your Father; and to my God, and your God.**

18 Mary Magdalene came and told the disciples that she had seen the Lord, and that he had spoken these things unto her.

19 Then the same day at evening, being the first day of the week, when the doors were shut where the disciples were assembled for fear of the Jews, came Jesus and stood in the midst, and saith unto them, **Peace be unto you.**

20 And when he had so said, he shewed unto them his hands and his side. Then were the disciples glad, when they saw the Lord.

21 Then said Jesus to them again, **Peace be unto you: as my Father hath sent me, even so Send I you.**

22 And when he had said this, he breathed on them, and saith unto them, **Receive ye the Holy Ghost:**

23 **Whose soever sins ye remit, they are remitted unto them; and whose soever sins ye retain, they are retained.**

24 But Thomas, one of the twelve, called Didymus, was not with them when Jesus came.

25 The other disciples therefore said unto him, We have seen the Lord. But he said unto them, Except I shall see in his hands the print of the nails, and put my finger into the print of the nails, and thrust my hand into his side, I will not believe.

26 And after eight days again his disciples were within, and Thomas with them: then came Jesus, the doors being shut, and stood in the midst, and said, **Peace be unto you.**

27 Then saith he to **Thomas, Reach hither thy finger, and behold my hands; and reach hither thy hand, and thrust it into my side: and be not faithless, but believing.**

28 And Thomas answered and said unto him, My Lord and my God.

29 Jesus saith unto him, **Thomas, because thou hast seen me, thou hast believed: blessed are they that have not seen, and yet have believed.**

30 And many other signs truly did Jesus in the presence of his disciples, which are not written in this book:

31 But these are written, that ye might believe that Jesus is the Christ, the Son of God; and that believing ye might have life through his name.

THE GOSPEL OF JOHN   CHAPTER 21

Jesus appears to the disciples at the sea of Tiberias. He says to Peter: 'Feed my sheep'. He foretells Peter's martyrdom and John's translation.

1 AFTER these things Jesus shewed himself again to the disciples at the sea of Tiberias; and on this wise shewed he himself.

2 There were together Simon Peter, and Thomas called Didymus, and Nathanael of Cana in Galilee, and the sons of Zebedee, and two other of his disciples.

3 Simon Peter saith unto them, I go a fishing. They say unto him, We also go with thee. They went forth, and entered into a ship immediately; and that night they caught nothing.

4 But when the morning was now come, Jesus stood on the shore: but the disciples knew not that it was Jesus.

5 Then Jesus saith unto them, **Children, have ye any meat?** They answered him, No.

6 And he said unto them, **Cast the net on the right side of the ship, and ye shall find**. They cast therefore, and now they were not able to draw it for the multitude of fishes.

7 Therefore that disciple whom Jesus loved saith unto Peter, It is the Lord. Now when Simon Peter heard that it was the Lord, he girt his fisher's coat unto him, (for he was naked,) and did cast himself into the sea.

8 And the other disciples came in a little ship; (for they were not far from land, but as it were two hundred cubits,) dragging the net with fishes.

9 As soon then as they were come to land, they saw a fire of coals there, and fish laid thereon, and bread.

10 Jesus saith unto them, **Bring of the fish which ye have now caught.**

11 Simon Peter went up, and drew the net to land full of great fishes, an hundred and fifty and three: and for all there were so many, yet was not the net broken.

12 Jesus saith unto them, **Come and dine.** And none of the disciples durst ask him, Who art thou? knowing that it was the Lord.

13 Jesus then cometh, and taketh bread, and giveth them, and fish likewise.

14 This is now the third time that Jesus shewed himself to his disciples, after that he was risen from the dead.

15 So when they had dined, Jesus saith to Simon Peter, **Simon, son of Jonas, lovest thou me more than these?** He saith unto him, Yea, Lord; thou knowest that I love thee. He saith unto him, **Feed my lambs.**

16 He saith to him again the second time, **Simon, son of Jonas, lovest thou me?** He saith unto him, Yea, Lord; thou knowest that I love thee. He saith unto him, **Feed my sheep.**

17 He saith unto him the third time, **Simon, son of Jonas, lovest thou me?** Peter was grieved because he said unto him the third time, **Lovest thou me?** And he said unto him, Lord, thou knowest all things; thou knowest that I love thee. Jesus saith unto him, **Feed my sheep.**

18 **Verily, verily, I say unto thee, When thou wast young, thou girdedst thyself, and walkedst whither thou wouldest: but when thou shalt be old, thou shalt stretch forth thy hands, and another shall gird thee, and carry thee whither thou wouldest not.**

19 This spake he, signifying by what death he should glorify God. And when he had spoken this, he saith unto him, **Follow me.**

20 Then Peter, turning about, seeth the disciple whom Jesus loved following; which also leaned on his breast at supper, and said, Lord, which is he that betrayeth thee?

21 Peter seeing him saith to Jesus, Lord, and what shall this man do?

22 Jesus saith unto him, **If I will that he tarry till I come, what is that to thee? follow thou me.**

23 Then went this saying abroad among the brethren, that that disciple should not die: yet Jesus said not unto him, He shall not die; but, **If I will that he tarry till I come, what is that to thee?**

24 This is the disciple which testifieth of these things, and wrote these things: and we know that his testimony is true.

25 And there are also many other things which Jesus did, the which, if they should be written every one, I suppose that even the world itself could not contain the books that should be written. Amen.

Footnote (2) Bishop James' handout

"Would Jesus Christ do that?"

The following list is long and admittedly not exhaustive. The answers are plain unless qualified in certain situations. Satan's misery, wickedness, temptations and sins, all designed to make us unhappy, are found on the left in the first word or phrase. Jesus Christ's happiness, righteousness and lighted way are found on the right in the second word or phrase. Add your own concepts to this list because no doubt my list is not complete. I am definitely not perfect and have probably missed something important.

Aborting Life vs. Preserving Life and Pro-life Principles.

Alcoholism vs. Sobriety

Breaking the Speed Limit and Laws of the Road vs. Observing and Keeping the Speed Limit and Traffic Laws.

Committing Adultery and Fornication vs. Living the law of Chastity.

Indulging in and Addicting to Alcohol vs. A life of Sobriety.

Anger vs. Kindness and gentleness.

Animal cruelty vs. Kindness to Animals and support of Animal rights.

Apostasy vs. Faithful to Church Leaders and The Church.

Assaulting Behavior vs. Patient Non-threatening Behavior.

Atheism and Agnosticism vs. God fearing.

Avoiding Church vs. Attending Church.

Bad vs. Good.

Betrayal vs. Honorable Support of Family, Friends, Neighbors, and Country.

Battery vs. Forbearance and Protection of Others.

Calumny and Slander vs. Honoring Others with Praise and Good Words.

Cheating vs. Honesty.

Child Abuse vs. Loving Protection of Children.

Coercion and Force vs. Respect for Each Person's Choice and Right to Choose.

Covetousness and Greed vs. Respect For That Which Belongs to Another Person.

Cowardice vs. Bravery.

Criticizing Dignitaries vs. Praising and Honoring Dignitaries.

Criticizing Family, Friends, and Others vs. Praising and Honoring Family, Friends, and Others.

Living in Darkness vs. Living in the Light of Christ.

Day of Work, Sin and Pleasure vs. Keeping the Sabbath day holy.

Deceiving Others vs. Being Truthful.

Despondent vs. Hopeful.

Destructive vs. Building

Disassociating Oneself from Others vs. Associating with Others.

Dishonesty vs. Honesty.

Disintegrity vs. Integrity.

Disobedience vs. Obedience.

Disorderly vs. Orderly.

Disrespect vs. Respect.

Divorce vs. Marriage.

Doubtful and Fearful vs. Faithful and Confident.

Draft Dodging vs. Patriotic.

Drug Addiction vs. Self-control.

Egotism, Pride, Hatred, and Anger vs. Humility.

Embezzlement, Waste, Debt, and Usury vs. Fiscal Honesty, Integrity and Debt Free.

Envy and Enmity vs. Seeking the Well Being of Others.

Evil vs. Good.

Falsehoods vs. Telling the Truth.

Fault Finding and Slander vs. Finding and Bringing Out the Best in Others.

Fearful vs. Hopeful.

Fighting against God the Father and His Son vs. Helping The Father and The Son achieve Their Work of Bringing to Pass the Immortality and Eternal Life of Men, Women and Children.

Following False, Unrighteous Counselors and Prophets vs. Following True and Righteous Counselors and Prophets.

Foolish vs. Being Wise.

Forcing Others vs. Allowing Freedom of Choice.

Fornicating vs. Being Pure and Chaste.

Gang Relationships vs. Avoidance of Gangs.

Genocide, Politicide, Policide, Ethnic Cleansing, Infanticide, Abortion, Hate Crimes and Other Crimes Against Humanity vs. Love of The Unborn, Children, Men and Women of All Races, Persuasions, Families, and Religions.

Gluttony vs. Moderation in Food Coupled with Appropriate Fasting.

Greed vs. Enough for One's Needs and Some Wants.

Hate and Disrespect Crimes vs. Love & Respect for Others Regardless of Race, Religion, or Persuasion.

Hatred vs. Love.

Hell as Focus vs. Heaven as Focus.

High Minded and Proud vs. Humble and Self-deprecating.

Horror vs. Up-lifiting and Enlightening.

Illicit Sex vs. Licit Sex Only Within the Bonds of Marriage of a Man and Woman.

Illicit Drugs vs. Proper use of Drugs in Healing.

Immodest vs. Modest.

Inhospitable vs. Hospitable.

Ingrate and Ingratitude vs. Person of Gratitude.

Impatient vs. Patient.

Incivility vs. Civility.

Infidelity vs. Fidelity.

Insider Trading vs. Fair dealing.

Intimidating vs. Non-threatening.

Irreverent vs. Reverent.

Jealousy and Envy vs. Not Threatened by and Honoring Others.

Love of Satan vs. Love of God The Father.

Love of Satan vs. The Pure love of Christ.

Love of Satan vs. Love of the Holy Ghost and Gifts of the Spirit.

Lust vs. Love.

Miserly and Stingy vs. Giving and Philanthropy.

Morose vs. Of Good Cheer.

Murderous vs. Protective of Life.

Non-compliance with government and IRS Regulations vs. Meticulous Compliance with government and IRS Regulations.

Non-compliance with Law vs. Meticulous Compliance with Law.

Non-compliance with SEC regulations vs. Compliance with SEC regulations.

Obesity Eating vs. Eating and Exercising to be Trim and Fit.

Pain Inflicting vs. Seeking the Comfort, Joy and Pleasure of others.

Pessimism vs. Optimism

Playing the Hypocrite vs. Avoiding Hypocrisy as the Plague it is.

Pleasure At Most if not All Cost vs. Moderation.

Pornography and Immodesty vs. Respect for the Female and Male Body and Sexuality.

Prayerless vs. Prayerful.

Proud vs. Humble.

Profane Swearing Conversation vs. Godlike Conversation.

Reclusive vs. Inclusive.

Refusal to Serve Others vs. Willingness to Serve Others.

Respecter of a Person's Status, Clothing, Cars, Riches and Wealth vs. Respecter of Each Person as a Human Being and as God's Child – no respecter of persons.

Road and "Line" Rage vs. Patience While Driving or Waiting for Others.

Sad and Depressed vs. Happy and Optimistic.

Selfish vs. Unselfish and Giving.

Self-righteous vs. Humble.

Sex abuse vs. Respect for the Body and Life and Sexuality.

Shouting, Noise, and Confusion vs. Quiet and Orderly.

Shunning the Aged and Elderly vs. Visiting and Helping the Aged and Elderly.

Shunning the Poor and Needy vs. Visiting and Helping the Poor and Needy.

Shunning the Sick and Afflicted vs. Visiting the Helping and Healing the Sick and Afflicted.

Shunning Those in Prison vs Visiting Those in Prison

Sickness mentality vs. Carrying a Mentality of Health.

Sinning vs. Righteousness in Keeping God's Commandments.

Slothful vs. Diligent Work and Industry.

Speedily Down to Hell vs. Speedily to Paradise and Heaven.

Stingy vs. Giving.

Stupid vs. Right Acquisition and Use of Knowledge, understanding, and wisdom.

Swearing and Taking God's Name in Vain vs. Civil language and Reverence for God's Name.

Taking vs. Giving.

Taking the Names of God the Father and His Son and Sacred Things In Vain vs. Honoring the Names of God the Father and His Son and Sacred Things.

Thievery vs. Respect for the Property of Others.

Using Tobacco vs. Avoiding Tobacco like the Cancer Plague it is.

Ugliness vs Focusing on Beauty.

Uncheerful vs. Cheerful.

Unconsecrated to God vs. Consecrated to God.

Unfit vs. Fit.

Unjustified vs. Justified.

Unhealthy vs. Healthy.

Unholy vs. Holy.

Unkind vs. Kind.

Unlawful vs. Lawful.

Unpraiseworthy vs. Praiseworthy.

Unsanctified vs. Sanctified.

Unthankful vs. Thankful.

Untruthful vs. Truthful.

Unrighteous vs. Righteous.

Unvirtuous vs. Virtuous.

Violation of Law vs. Adherence to Law.

Violence and Abuse vs. Kindness, Gentleness, and Peace.

War vs. Peace.

Wickedness vs. Righteousness.

Willful Failure to File and Pay Taxes vs. Willing filing and Payment of Taxes,

Worldly vs. Not worldly.

Footnote (3) "According to Andrew Walsh's "Church, Lies, and Polling Data," from Religion in the News, Fall 1998, Volume 1, Number 2, The Leonard E. Greenberg Center for the Study of Religion in Public Life, Trinity College, Hartford, Connecticutt, the Gallup and other statistical studies, most of which are self-reporting, conclude that 40% of Americans say they attended Church in the last seven days. Fact is the article goes on to say that this number 40% may well be a sham number since self-reporting statistics are notoriously inaccurate. More careful studies that included actual counting suggest that this number is closer to 20%. In any case, the number of Americans who worship in Church on Sunday is probably well below 40%. At 20%, this would suggest that out of a population of 296 million, only 59 million worship in Church on Sunday. That would mean 237 million Americans did not attend Church. Is there a mighty room for improvement? No doubt. Would Jesus attend Church regularly?

And a couple of definitions you probably picked up on, but on the off chance you didn't: A bishop in The Church of Jesus Christ of Latter-day Saints (the Mormons) is like a reverend or pastor. A ward is like a parish. A stake is like a diocese. The first principles of the gospel are, faith in the Lord Jesus Christ, repentance, baptism by immersion for the remission of sins, and laying on of hand for the gift of The Holy Ghost.

About The Author

Richard Linford is an active member of The Church of Jesus Christ of Latter-day Saints (The Mormons). He served as a bishop in the Church. He is a businessman, Attorney at Law, writer, artist and sometime golfer. He works at being a good husband, dad, grandpa, and neighbor.

The Author's Postscript

We are children of God the Father and His Son Jesus is the Christ. I have written this short story about Bishop James and Mary Thomas, have appended the New Testament Gospel of John with the words of Jesus Christ in bold, have titled this book "Would Jesus Christ Do That? is the first question!" hoping such may be of some Christian influence in motivating each of us where necessary to repent, change our ways and improve our lives in preparation for those certain and exciting eventualities of death, at which time we face a partial judgment, and the prophesied "great" and "dreadful" Second Coming of Jesus Christ, with His attendant thousand year millennial reign on earth..

I dedicate this small work to my family and to you regardless of your religion or beliefs. I pray God will bless you and your family with the richest of His blessings. Having read these thoughts, I hope you have a better appreciation for the truth that God's richest blessings of peace, happiness, and joy come from keeping His commandments and serving others. May you find the thoughts in this little book provocative and helpful. I also share my optimistic view of the future. "Be not afraid" and "be of good cheer" are comforting words of Our Savior. I wish you great health, happiness, and prosperity!

Would Jesus Christ Do That? is the first question! What Would Jesus Do? is the second question!

Richard Linford

A couple of websites you may find interesting include: www.lds.org and www.mormon.org

The Author's Blog is http://jesus-isthechrist.blogspot.com/

See www.amazon.com for added copies.

A Sweetwater Book Company publication

Book of Mormon 2 Nephi Chapter 25 verse 20. And now, my brethren, I have spoken plainly that ye cannot err. And as the Lord God liveth that brought Israel up out of the land of Egypt, and gave unto Moses power that he should heal the nations after they had been bitten by the poisonous serpents, if they would cast their eyes unto the serpent which he did raise up before them, and also gave him power that he should smite the rock and the water should come forth; yea, behold I say unto you, that as these things are true, and **as the Lord God liveth, there is none other name given under heaven save it be this Jesus Christ, of which I have spoken, whereby man can be saved.**

Book of Mormon Helaman Chapter 5 verse12. **And now, my sons, remember, remember that it is upon the rock of our Redeemer, who is Christ, the Son of God, that ye must build your foundation;** that when the devil shall send forth his mighty winds, yea, his shafts in the whirlwind, yea, when all his hail and his mighty storm shall beat upon you, it shall have no power over you to drag you down to the gulf of misery and endless wo, because of the rock upon which ye are built, which is a sure foundation, a foundation whereon if men build they cannot fall.

Would Jesus Christ Do That?

is the first question!

Richard W. Linford

What Would Jesus Christ Do?

is the second question!

Richard W. Linford

www.ingramcontent.com/pod-product-compliance
Lightning Source LLC
LaVergne TN
LVHW081325060426
835511LV00011B/1867